Up North

Up North

by

WILLIAM H. HULL

For copies, try your bookstore first.
Available to them through their distributors.
Please give the bookstore the identifying ISBN number shown on this page.

You may also order single copies from the author/publisher
at the address shown above. Send cover price plus shipping and handling
charges of $2.25 *per book*. Charges subject to change.

Cover photo features Scott S. Froemming, Crystal, Minnesota.
See story herein titled "Hunting Until Nearly Dark Pays Off."

TABLE OF CONTENTS

Introduction

Dear Dad:

You'll be surprised at what we had for dinner today. Not your favorite pork roasted as Mother always does it, with the succulent fat left in the kitchen for you to have a few bites of your truly favorite. As you grew older, I always wondered how your body could assimilate that fat, when experts have been telling us for years that fat is verboten. But you flourished in spite of it, probably because of your hard physical work that stepped on the potential damage the fat could do.

Well, we had rabbit. Not the wild kind but a poor domesticated thing from a cage, extremely clean and well dressed, frozen at our supermarket. Carol bought it after I had agreed that I would cook it for us—which means fry it in this house.

I was hesitant to tackle *hassenpfeffer* again after so many years, but planned to fry it like chicken, as I've seen Mother do so great many times. It still had to be cut into smaller pieces, even though Carol had left the big rear legs in the package to remain in the freezer compartment.

It was good but not fabulous; rabbit is such a solid meat it doesn't fry too well, which is probably why the Germans learned to make *hassenpfeffer* in the first place. That way it is more moist and a gravy is supplied with it, as you know. And, of course, that little pinch of red pepper doesn't do any harm. I'll bet the Germans also cooked it with sauerkraut.

To digress a moment, I was thinking earlier today how in early America there were "meat hunters" who supplied meat markets or general stores with skinned rabbits to hang up for sale, displaying them much like Chinese stores display duck carcasses. Mother, very wisely, would have wondered how clean they were. Of course, I never saw rabbits hanging outside at a meat market. Maybe you didn't either because that was a long time ago, the picture kept alive by the movies for people like me.

But we got our own share of rabbits, didn't we? You, mainly. You would take that big old blunderbuss of yours, that twelve-gauge, with its barrel of twisted Damascus steel. That barrel always scared the hell out of me after you once told me it couldn't

take the heavy loads of modern shells and was considered dangerous. I always feared the barrel would explode. To my dying
day I'll carry the guilt that I didn't buy you a more modern, safe
shotgun. The son who bought his Dad a brand-new Browning or
something just as good. Shame on me. Money was tight, but I
still should have done it. I just didn't think, I guess, because it
was dangerous when either of us used it.

Of course I didn't have a shotgun of my own either; I either
used yours or my new Ward's .22 rifle, which was more of a toy
anyway.

Rabbit and squirrel meat were really staples during the De-
pression, weren't they, for a lot of us in rural or semirural areas?
You could really stop a running rabbit, Dad, with that gun of
yours, and Mother could get a squirrrel with the rifle. You must
have been proud of her ability because many times you praised
her for being able to hit a squirrel in the eye, even when it was
high up in a tree. Did you teach her that skill? It was an unusual
ability for a short little Irish woman.

This letter is getting too long but I do want to share something with you. When working on my book *The Dirty Thirtie,* I
was referred to a black woman in one of those western suburbs of
St. Louis. We had a nice long talk in her home. She had been
noted all her life as a woman who could cook any wild game.
People would bring her odd animals no one ever ate, ask her to
cook it, and she'd produce a very tasty dish. She mentioned
"things like possum and muskrat," saying they were very tasty if
you could just find and remove the scent glands. "I think I
cooked and we ate about everything except skunk, but I'd never
try that because the stink was already on the meat."

She was also very proud of the memory of her husband. He
had kept them in meat by killing rabbits, of which there were
plenty in the thirties. "But you know," she went ahead, "he killed
them with a special stick he made and called it something like a
'humper.' He would throw it at a rabbit and hit him everytime."

When I asked her, with great innocence, why he didn't use a
gun, she replied, "Why, Mr. Hull, blacks weren't allowed to own
a gun in those days. Even if you had one, no one would sell you
shells."

I'd never heard that before, had you, Dad? It's one of those things we probably need to know. Damned! We were cruel to blacks weren't we?

No wonder I like to hunt. I certainly was raised knowing a lot about hunting. As a boy I got to hunt with you and a few times with Uncle Pat[1]. I remember that duck-hunting lodge (shack) your younger brothers, Pat, Seb, Roy, and probably brother-in-law, John, built on the bluff overlooking the Missouri River. After being on the river duck hunting, I well remember trying to climb that heavily overgrown hill straight up to the shack while carrying Pat's very heavy ten horse cast-iron outboard motor. As I slipped and slid up that muddy bank, Pat gently relieved me of the weight, sensing that it was too heavy for a stringbean teenager like me. On another occasion I was quail hunting with several of those uncles. Spread out across a field, we slowly advanced. My first quail hunt. I was at the left of Pat when a covey broke in front of us and I waited for no one. Bang! Bang!

Pat was astounded.

"Damnit, Bill, you just beat me to the draw Where did you learn to shoot like that?"

Those were praise and much-appreciated words to a kid. Great Uncle Arth would have said, "Damnmeeee, boy." That felt good.

I also did a little goose hunting on the Missouri, married Carol in 1943, and soon moved to Minnesota, and started deer hunting.

Boy, was that a switch.

As you know, Dad, I was a babe in toyland. I had no clothes appropriate for Minnesota winters.

Do you remember me telling you how well that Virginia, Minnesota, gang took me over? How dumbfounded they were that I came there in lightweight khaki ducks for Missouri river and woods hunting? Andy and Lucille[2] scrounged around in their family's hunting gear and got something on me for warmth, and Lucille sewed patches of red cloth all over my clothes to meet the law's requirement.

Shoes? I think I had leather boots in which my feet almost

froze, partly because they were always wet. Believe me, the next year I had some appropriate clothing.

And someone loaned me a rifle.

With all of that mismatched gear, how did I ever manage to down two running yearlings who came zipping past my deer stand? Dumb luck, I suppose.

All of those years of rifle practice to qualify me for Junior National Rifle Association awards (yes, even a Junior instructor) must have been very helpful because at least I could swing a rifle at a moving target.

So I've hunted in Minnesota ever since, with an occasional jaunt like that Arkansas trip to get a Black Russian wild boar—and now I'm accumulating deer stories for a new book—my eighth, Dad.

Now that I've written this long (nay, very long) letter, what do I do with it? Of course, you've both been gone for many years, Dad for seven and Mother for twenty-nine, and I've become an old man.

But we think of you a lot, Carol and I; your granddaughters, Judy and Pauline; your great granddaughters, Ingrid and Erica.

Thanks for having been there most of my life.

BILL

1. Pat or Clarence Hull, Bill's father's youngest brother.
2. Einer and Lucille Anderson, Carol's sister and brother-in-law.

Up North

It was cold up in that tree near Cook, Minnesota, in the area Twin Cities residents call "Up North." Minneapolis and St. Paul people have lots of ties with residents of those northern towns because many of them were born and raised there. That area, also known as part of the Range, includes towns on the Mesabi Iron Range, sources of underground iron ore deposits of which zillions of tons were brought to the surface, moved by train or truck to the ports of Duluth/Superior, and transported by ore boats to the smelting cities of the East. There that ore became automobiles, turbines, and other heavy equipment.

Those towns, like Hibbing, Virginia, Coleraine, Grand Rapids, and Mountain Iron were targeted desiginations by the influx of Scandinavian and Irish miners and woodsmen.

Northern Wisconsin and Michigan were similar. In fact, it was the Welsh settlers in Michigan who contributed, among other things, the pasty (pronounced with a short "a"), the portable meat pie which became a basic food of the area. Somewhat like a chicken pot pie, they are made of chunks of beef (even venison), carrots, potatoes, and rutabagas, cooked within a circle of pie-like dough to seal in the natural juices. Transported to the mines or the woods in a lunch pail, they were warmed, perhaps over a miner's lamp, and were a healthy, satisfying meal. Not to be confused with a pasty (long "a") which is an ornament worn by a stripper.

But back to the story. How did I happen to be up in that tree stand on a subzero winter morning?

It was November 1943 and this young man from Missouri had married a Ranger from Virginia three months earlier, met a group of friendly middle-aged teachers from the Range, and accepted an invitation to join their annual hunting party in November.

So the newlyweds drove from Missouri to Minnesota to start the ritual of deer hunting Up North. The second half of the ritual was the goal of coming out of the event alive.

Although I had hunted for years, I had no appropriate clothing that first year. One of the group loaned me two pairs of long johns, one cotton, one part wool. I bought a special red hunting cap and choppers, those finger-saving mittens made of heavy horsehide with removeable wool interliner mittens, called "choppers" because woodcutters adopted them for the long winter days of working in the woods.

The real problem concerned outer clothing and boots. My lightweight khaki bird-hunting clothing was a threat to my life and illegal. My calf-high rubber boots could have cost me my feet. The women in my family sewed pieces of red flannel over my khakis because red was the required color in those days (orange now). They also scrounged up old worn-out shirts and jackets to wear underneath it all. I remember being so bundled I could barely move and yet so cold I shook, a situation which only became worse when I tried walking through the woods, sweating under the many layers. Then, when I stopped, I learned what cold really was all about.

At that point, I was asking myself what the hell I was doing there, particularly when sitting up in that tree with the wind whipping through my thin jacket and porous open-weave wool shirt.

Remember that the fancy, all-purpose jackets for outdoor sports just didn't exist in those days. If one were truly lucky one had a jacket stuffed with goose down, which probably had been saved by goose hunters.

The other day I saw a lady from Denver wearing a Bronco's jacket in Minnesota. It would have been the envy of every deer hunter fifty years ago, except that its vibrant colors would have attracted some of the nimrods wandering through the woods to take a shot at it.

To protect me and, hopefully, to keep me alive, the gang assigned me to a good stand, a spot I really appreciated and enjoyed.

So there I sat, freezing to death, shaking violently, with a powerful rifle balanced across my knees, constantly fighting off an aggressive whiskey jack, which wanted to eat all of my salted-in-the-shell peanuts and cussed me by the hour.

Now every hunter on a stand knows that he must be sharp-eyed and quiet. He does not cough. He does not call to a team member whom he suspects is over the next ridge. He does not bring along a small transistor radio to listen to the weather and news. He knows that the game can hear the broadcast much better than he can. He does not doze and fall from the tree with a loaded rifle. Above all, he does not permit himself to think of food, coffee, or whiskey, and then yield to the temptation to slide to the ground and slip back to the hunting shack.

No sirree.

Not even for a good bowl of hot soup. Not even to build the fire in the stove to make it warm for others when they chicken out and sneak home! He knows he just cannot do those things.

No. He stays put.

So he just keeps sitting there, wondering, "Will I ever see a deer?"

Sometimes he will.

Sometimes he won't.

When he hears a noise, he watches the trail carefully, cap shading eyes from the lowering sun, gun cocked and ready, safety still on, awaiting a deer.

Then he hears it. A twig snaps. Leaves rustle among the snow. You watch the trail . . . and soon out it steps.

It's a rabbit.

But he's coming up the trail, not down the trail where you are looking. He stumbles along hesitantly.

Or, on a slim chance, it's a friend, like Andy, who steps out in the open, waves a hello and comes to the base of your tree to ask quietly, "Do you have any red toilet paper?"

I haven't so he moves on up the trail. Soon he'll be looking for moss, no matter how cold and wet it is.

In the meantime, those whiskey jacks are cawing like their cousins, the blue jays in town. They're spreading the alarm all over the country, and causing three or four bucks with record racks to run full out for Canada, where we'll never see them again.

It looked like it would be a complete bust for me that first year.

Until late afternoon when the sun's rays were fully in my eyes and it was cooling off for the night.

I jumped (perhaps "flinched" would be a better word) when into my small clearing came two deer running nearly side by side, moving fast. I didn't have time to see whether they were bucks or does but had to shoot quickly or they'd be gone.

Fixing my sight on the first one, I fired BLAM behind his front leg, swung my rifle to the second one quickly, and went BLAM again.

The smoke cleared, either in the air or in my foggy mind, as I looked down and across the clearing, trying to find the two deer. I didn't see them any place.

Were they gone?

I had missed both shots.

Damn!

Then I saw them. Both were down in the clearing, not too visible among the high, dead grass. A third BLAM quieted the one still thrashing.

I had killed both of them.

On my first hunt I had filled out for two of us with two yearlings in fine condition. My quail-and-duck-hunting shooting had paid off in spades—no—deer, not spades.

So there was nothing left to do except to dress out the two yearlings and use my rope to pull them back to camp.

I wasn't considered such a raw recruit after that. I'd passed the test.

WILLIAM H. HULL

(Written January 23, 1995, as first effort on the book Up North.*)*

The Guy Who Drowned His Deer

It was Saturday morning in deer season 1944. My roomate, Ed, and I headed after deer at 7 A.M. wearing at least four layers of clothing. We met Ed's friend Steve at his home near Windom, Minnesota, and started our hunting by going to a nearby draw where I dropped Ed and Steve and then went ahead about one-fourth of a mile to look where we thought deer might head out from the timber.

It was colder than anything, standing in that extreme cold waiting for something to happen.

I had a Winchester Super-X Model One I had picked up at Fin and Feather. Not only had I never shot it, that also meant it wasn't sighted in yet.

There, in the cold, I was glad I had gone to the Fleetway store the night before and purchased a full-faced blaze-orange stocking cap. Now I had to face a rather strong wind and that cap stopped the wind on my face. All I saw was a couple of rabbits jump out of a brush pile, while Ed flushed six pheasants. No deer came our way.

When Ed came by my stand, he said I looked ready to knock off a 7-Eleven store. So we left that spot and drove around for some time to find another good spot for me to post. As we moved around we saw pickups and 4x4s all filled with guys wearing blaze orange, which we could see through the vehicle windows. I envied them, thinking that a blaze orange body suit would feel great right now. Also it would make me feel secure. With all those hunters running around, I wanted to be sure they saw me as a person before shooting.

It was a long east-west road, running along the Black Diamond Road. Just off that road was a short little lane that went down to the ridge-out area. In the meantime, I was getting very cold. My feet were quite painful.

Since my feet were nearly frozen solid, I decided to get some lunch in our shack and then go get my buck.

Later, I stood on the north side of the creek and waited. It was about ten o'clock in the morning and as cold as I ever experienced. My toes were beginning to freeze, so I started doing excercises with them—up, down, around in circles, anything to warm them.

I wanted to cross the creek but it was about thirty feet across with a bunch of branches in the water. The real job was to find a better crossing. I was afraid I'd fall in that icy water and drop my gun. The bank on the other side was about ten feet high. Timber ran across my view and stopped about sixty feet south where there was a large flat field.

Over there, across that field, looked like a perfect spot for a deer stand. I looked at that cold water and decided to stay where I was and to exercise my toes to keep them from freezing so badly that amputation would be necessary. I was miserable.

The ice on the creek was gradually breaking up, sounding like something coming thrrough the brush. A deer? It was a very peaceful scene except that now and then I'd hear a plop or crunch of ice and nearly wet my pants. This wouldn't be good when wearing four layers of clothes. I stood there about thirty minutes exercising and getting spooked by noises. Then something moved to my left.

Damn! It was a buck with a doe trailing behind him. They were walking fast, weaving in and out among the trees. They were now right across the creek where all along I had thought I should be posted, but I just couldn't find a way across that wide creek.

If I'd only crossed when I had a chance some time ago.

Straight across and to the right from where I was standing was a clearing they were about to enter. I drew a bead and held it. I don't think I took a breath from the time I first saw the buck until I pulled the trigger.

The clearing was about thirty-five yards from me. I aimed just behind the front leg as I had been instlructed. I pulled; I missed! How could I miss?

If it were anywhere else he would have been long gone, but his front legs slid on the ice as he struggled to get up and get out of there. The icy rocks and turf slowed him considerably. I fired two more shots and thought the second one had hit him. Actually it hit a little south of home, as I learned later.

I finally took a breath and they were both gone. My heart was pounding and I was full of adrenaline. After the first shot, the buck did hesitate for a second as if he were hit, but then he took off. I thought I missed him totally. How could I have missed? I was now trying to figure out how to get across that creek so I could check for blood.

I decided to set my gun down when Ted yelled, "Did you get one?" I decided to cross the creek on the old limbs and have a quick look around. I'd just gotten across the water and was trying to find a low spot on the bank to get back up to ground level when Ed came panting up on the other side. I said, "I don't think so, but I'm going to check for blood."

"Any blood?" Ed didn't seem happy and was grumbling. I went down through the right and saw blood and hair behind where I had shot. I yelled the information back to Ed and he yelled back, "You must have hit him." I thought I'd look just a little further, just to see if the blood trail continued. I was pretty excited and I guess I lost control, knowing I was on the trail of a buck I really had hit and worried that I hadn't gotten a good enough hit to put him down, that he would go off a long way. If the blood trail would continue, I would see a pretty large pool of blood, then just a spray once in a while, then a puddle again. His trail was weaving in and around the basic trail and brush. I'd gone about forty yards when I looked up ahead from the trail I was following—and there he was.

He was about fifteen yards ahead of me, lying down. I stopped and he flung his head around, saw me, and jumped as he took off. That's when I learned what all hunters know: NEVER, NEVER, NEVER LEAVE YOUR GUN BEHIND. I had this sinking feeling in my gut that said you dumb shit.

Now, today with the training I have received from seasoned hunters, I would go back to where I'd left my gun or had Ed and Steve help me trail the deer. If the three of us had been able to trail as a team, I realize that would have been no assurance that the deer wouldn't have been lost anyway. But NOOOOOO!. I decided to go on. After following that blood, I was pumped. I didn't know why I was doing this, but it seemed like the thing to do at the time. After trailing another fifty yards I came upon a fallen tree, like a lean-to, and there he was again trying to die in peace. OOOOOPS! The deer got up and away he went. Another easy shot, and me without a gun. Should I go back now for help, or go on by myself? I'd gone close to one-fourth mile, wending along the creek. What the heck . . . I'll go a few more yards, following that rough bush along the creek.

Later I calculated that I had gone only about a quarter of a mile but in that creekside brush it was very hard moving. Later when I had gone at least one-half mile, I came up to him again—the third time. He was just standing on that steep cliff or bank about ten feet above the creek.

As soon as I saw him I decided to keep moving my feet to help get them warm, so I stood there in place, moving my feet up and down wondering what to do next.

What a sight. A man marching in place trying to convince a fine eight-point buck that he was no enemy—and the hunter without a gun.

I guess one does weird things in situations like this. I remember looking down at my hands as if by some miracle my gun would suddenly be there. It wasn't, so I called myself a few more cute names. Apparently the deer got bothered with my dance routine, and simply moved on.

Down the ten-foot bank into the water he went. He almost reached the other bank before he slowed down, stopped a few times, then swayed a few times before he fell over. I kept yelling for Steve or Ed to help me load the animal into the van and get it back to camp. After yelling my two buddies' names for a while, with no response, I could see that was getting me nowhere. I also worried that the deer might take off again down the trail, for someone else to stop and claim him. I wanted that deer.

So I decided I had to cross the creek at some point and come back for the deer, which was nearer to the far side where we had our vehicles. I knew I had to do something soon.

I was still yelling for Ed and Steve, but my voice surely couldn't carry the half mile or so to them. But the deer didn't seem to be bothered by my calling for assistance. He just stood there in that very cold water. I felt sorry for him and wished I'd had my gun to put him out of his pain.

I was still very much concerned that I'd lose the deer for some reason. To the north of me, across the creek, were about eighty acres of woodland near the Black Diamond Road. I watched that road through the trees for a time, hoping to see Ed and Steve in the truck, but no luck. So I crossed the creek to get a little closer to the deer and on his same level, since he was standing closer to that far bank. All of this time I was thinking that I might have to use my knife to put him down.

I could see no easy route to get to him. No shallows, no brush to walk atop, just water. And I couldn't help thinking it would have been a perfect heart/lung shot. There was a rather heavy seven-foot tree limb nearby, so I took it with me toward the deer, intending to get it into his rack and force his head into the water. Boy was that water cold inside my boots; it was up to my thighs. The deer tried to move away, but he had sunk so deeply in the mud of the creek it was hard for both of us.to move in that predicament.

I thought "Just push down on him and drown him quickly to get it over with." That seemed to be the most humane thing to do *at the time*.

I don't know what I was thinking about but I could hardly believe I was doing this—so I let go of the branch and grabbed his rack. I was pushing down on his head and had him down quite a while when he bucked and I lost my grip on the rack. He quickly took another breath, which I was sorry to see; I didn't want this to take long for both of our sakes. I moved around to his left side, grabbed his rack again, pushed down and put my knee on his neck. We both were struggling strongly. My adrenaline was high and I feared that he would get a surge of reserve power and gore me, which was a definite possibility. Again, I wondered how I had put myself into this situation, wishing this combat were over and wanting my gun.

Then over my shoulder I caught a glimpse of blaze orange and thought Ed had showed up. I turned to look at him, but he was a complete stranger. When I first saw him he was standing there with his gun hanging in one hand and his mouth open to his chest. I'm sure I was a sight.

Later he told me that he had been standing there for about five minutes watching the battle. He had heard some noise down by the creek and had come through the woods to investigate. He'd thought it might be a deer downed in the creek and he'd get his trophy then and there.

I started babbling to him about having made a bad shot and having to chase the deer through the woods. He commented that one should never leave one's gun behind. I suppose he was one of those "seasoned hunters." He offered me his gun, but I declined, saying I was about done here anyway.

I went on about how I'd never go deer hunting again. I'm not sure that I said that because I was feeling so sorry for the deer or because I was so embarrassed.

I had been holding the deer's head under water for at least two minutes and thought that would be plenty of time. It must be all over now. I then started to pull him out of the water and even considered pulling him to the road. I was still at water level, which the reader will remember was ten feet lower than the surrounding ground level. I climbed out of that hole and started yelling for my buddies. Among other things, I really didn't know how to gut an animal but knew it must be done quickly.

I took my boots off and squeezed the icy water out of my socks, realizing that now I had to get that heavy deer up to level ground. How to do that? I sat on my butt and pulled the deer by its rack up to my waist, then scooting backwards repeated the whole process. Let me assure you that a 175-pound dead animal is very, very heavy. I remember that he'd slide easily over the snow when I headed for the road with him.

I went looking for Ed and Steve whom I thought might be cruising the road looking for me. Sure enough, almost immediately they came by in the truck. Ed then told me that the hunter who had been watching me had talked with them, saying, "You'll never believe what I just saw." He told them he had seen a big guy down in the creek wrestling with a large buck. They knew it had to be me. They all got a big laugh about that. I prefer to call it *subduing* the deer.

Ed drove me to Fin and Feathers where they took my picture with the deer to put it on their trophy board. I don't think when you look at the photo that I'm the kind of a guy to leave his gun behind, but, on the other hand, how many hunters have their photo on that board with such a story to tell?

KEITH BARKALOW
Iowa City, Iowa

How to Cook an Elephant – or Maybe a Deer

Years ago we heard a couple of stories about cooking an elephant. One dealt with cooking the whole carcass and serving several thousand people with the meat. Another centered around making elephant ear sandwiches and the difficulty of obtaining those large buns to make the ear sandwiches.

When the hunter comes home with the venison, the spouse sometimes feels overwhelmed with the chore ahead. How do I cook this thing? Aren't you going to cut it up or have it cut up into decent size pieces? And, most of all, it comes down to the question of how do I handle this big hunk of venison roast? What the devil am I supposed to do with it?

Of course, it isn't hard to know what to do with steaks and chops. Just handle them about like you would beef. But a roast! What do I do—which was the question I first asked years ago, particularly from my sister, Lucille, eight years my senior, whose husband had been deer hunting for many years before Bill and I first met.

Lucille gave me some help and I soon learned to fix venison roast, which Bill raved and bragged about to his friends. Those were sweet words when I heard him say to a friend, "My Carol really knows how to fix a delicious venison roast, complete with potatoes and carrots, but most of all, she gets rid of any 'wild meat' taste."

Several people to whom we served it asked how to do it; so here are the secrets.

First, the hunter has to treat the animal correctly. After being shot, it must be bled, which means the blood must be drained from the carcass as quickly as possible and the meat must be kept cool. This means the carcass should be suspended from a tree limb, or a rope in camp, after having been gutted and perhaps washed out with water or snow, permitting it to drain well. Then it must be transported home in some careful way, most of all not on the fender of a car or truck where it gets heated by the nearby motor.

In our part of the country, experienced hunters either butcher the carcass themselves or take it to a nearby locker that offers butchering service. The meat is treated carefully, butchered, packaged, and flash frozen to cure it as fast as possible. Then one takes one of the frozen packages, perhaps a family-sized roast, and thaws it out at home.

Now, it should be treated much like a beef roast, but first all of the tallow and fat should be cut off and thrown away; much of the wild scent and taste are in the fat and, by getting rid of it, the cook can eliminate any unpleasant taste.

Brown slowy in a heavy pan.

Place the roast on foil in an oven-proof pan. The foil must be large enough to fold and enclose the meat later. The seasoning can be a personal preference. I use dry onion soup mix to season, plus about one-fourth cup of water, which I enclose with the foil.

Into the oven at 325 degrees for an hour per pound. The vegetables may be added the last hour: small onions, small redskinned potatoes cut in halves, medium carrots cut in fourths.

People like this roast. Don't be surprised if the family asks if there is more gravy.

Carol Hull

Conversations at the Lake

Cars overflowed from the small parking lot at the lake.

Guys lounged in lawn chairs in the back yard, on the sidewalk, all over the place, between the kitchen entrance to the house and the path out to the privy.

The crowd had gathered quickly when the word got around that Stella was cooking a big kettle of her great spaghetti—and that the door was open.

Empty plates stained with spaghetti sauce were everywhere. On the ground near chairs. On the picnic table.

Boy, Fred, Stella sure makes great spaghetti.

You ought to know. Ate at least a whole box yourself.

Yeah, but too much meat in the sauce.

You Eyetalians. You think you own spaghetti.

Well, we invented it.

No, I hear it was the Chinese.

Soon the conversation might get personal.

Well, who cares?

Yeah. Got any brandy, Fred? Beer?

Yes, a couple of bottles in that old radio cabinet in the living room.

I'll get them. A willing worker spoke up.

Now you guys take it easy. We don't want you getting so drunk you can't drive. (The womenfolk had now been heard from.)

Oh shut up, Marge.

More gab. More brandy. Time flies.

What's Perpich up to these days?

Haven't you heard? Pass the brandy.

It's gone. Where's the other bottle?

Now he's gonna make chopsticks for the Chinese. What a damn fool idea. By the time they get them to China they'll be so expensive they won't sell.

Doesn't matter. We'll waste another million trees and give jobs to some of us.

Yeah, but listen to my words. The jobs will all end up in the Cities and nothing for us here on the Range.

Hey, where's the brandy? Pass it along.

You better go easy on that stuff, Mike. You're getting red in the face.

I don't care. If you can't get loaded on a Sunday afternoon, sitting here in the sun, when can you?

Look at Allie over there—throwing up on the blueberries. Fred, you won't have any blueberries there for another year, at least.

Doesn't matter too much. She'd rather go to that field up the road and fight the bears to pick them. She can pick blueberries faster than any bear can scoop them up. Just one thing wrong, though.

What's that?

She can't outrun the bear.

Laugh. Laugh.

Damned! That spaghetti was great! But know something? I'm getting hungry again.

Me, too. Got any more brandy? Even the cheap stuff?

No, didn't anybody bring any? I've got a bottle in the pickup. I'll get it.

Hell's bells! That won't be enough for this crowd, particularly if the girls decide they want a drink too.

I'm thinking of what Pete said. I'm getting hungry, too. Got any steaks in the freezer, Fred?

Not here, but some good venison steaks in the freezer in town. From that young buck I got near Cook last fall. We could go get them.

Not me. I'm too drunk to drive that thirty miles round-trip.

No, but you'd eat a steak wouldn't you?

Damn right. Someone ought to go get them. Something to drink, too.

Who needs it? We're all pretty loaded now.

Yeah, but we gotta have something for the rest of the day.

Now five o'clock and time's ticking.

I'll go get the steaks, says Fred.

Pete speaks up—And I'll go along to get some brandy from my place. Liquor stores all closed today. It's Sunday.

Okay, get Stella and the girls to put some potatoes in the oven to bake. We'll be back in less than an hour. Someone build a charcoal fire in the grill. Everything's in the shed over there.

Fred, you're too drunk to drive.

Doubtful, but I'll drive fast to get it over. Mike, tell the girls what we're going to do . . . and get them going on the potatoes. I know we've got plenty of them. How many steaks, guys?

Looks like a dozen anyway.

Okay, we're gone.

An hour later.

We're back—steaks and booze.

Did you guys run right over the sheriff's patrol?

No, whizzed right on past them at the Sand Lake store.

Great! Gimmie the bottle. I'm about the only one here awake.

Okay, but take it easy. You want to be awake for the steaks soon.

While you fix the steaks, I'm gonna build a fire in your sauna. I've gotta sweat out some of this brandy.

Okay, says Fred, go ahead. We guys will all go together.

How about getting the gals to join us?

You crazy? My wife would never do that.

The way I hear it, your wife will never do anything.

Oh, shut up.

Later. Big, hot potatoes slathered with butter— and huge, tender venison steaks are all gone. Plates litter the area while shrill voices of the women come from the kitchen. Guys are either asleep, drunk, or bored in their chairs. The sun is going down.

Hey, what the hell. It's getting late. We gotta go.

Without a sauna? You're nuts. Let's go.

Mad rush to the sauna where guys sit on different levels to sweat it out, soaping and sweating to cleanse themselves.

Dammit. I'm getting sleepy. Let's get out of here. We really gotta go home now.

Yeah, us too. Thanks for a great day, Fred. We've really gotta get humping now. Take care.

A mad rush to run down the dock, jump into the lake, return to dress, rush away for home, to sleep and sleep.

Take care, guys. Drive carefully.

Goodbye . . . goodbye . . . goodbye.

ANONYMOUS

Free Loading Whiskey Jacks

Probably some well-informed birder could tell me where the Canada jay picked up its nickname as the whiskey jack. Maybe some gyppo made a pet out of the uninhibited wild bird, got him started stealing whiskey-laced food, and hence the name.

Whatever, it's a sure thing that any hunter who has ever sat in a tree stand in the northern tier knows this bird. Why not? When you are up in a tree, maybe fifteen to twenty feet above the ground, freezing cold, your fingers wishing for real choppers (those lined leather mittens) instead of gloves, when cold tears edge down your cheeks to turn to ice, when a sudden movement catches your peripheral vision just as few feet away in the tree, you see a bird. A bird! I'm looking for a deer, you think, and here is this crazy bird wanting to be friends—sort of.

Yes, there he sits, a beautiful bird the size and shape of our blue jay, only his coloring is a drab gray—much more a prison gray I thought, when first encountering the whiskey jack.

It was cold that first day I met the whiskey jack. At least ten below with a windchill that reached way down to hell and back. Estimated windchill of twenty or more below zero. Friends, if you aren't perfectly dressed in layers, that's awfully cold. Somewhere in that temperature range it is said that if you spit, the sputum would crack and freeze before it hits the ground. Being a true student, I had to try it. So I tried to work up enough spit to do the job.

Nothing. My mouth was too dry.

No spit.

I know, I thought. Think of a sweet, ripe orange, one of my favorite foods.

Immediately my mouth began to produce a little moisture. Not enough. Think again.

Succulent grapes!

Great! Here comes the spit.

I hawked, coughed, and produced a juicy spit, which I propelled down to the distant ground.

It froze! Really! I could see it bounce when it hit the ground, way down there.

Then, in hunger caused by my imagination, I turned to my stash. What had I brought along in my pockets?

Of course, this guy was predictible. I *always* brought peanuts in the shell because we had a good source of them from South Carolina and because they were so satisfying.

In the meantime the word went out to my friend, the W.J. And I knew Jack would get the word and would be present.

Yes, within five minutes he was there, close to my hand, watching carefully and talking to me. His attitude inferred that a handful of nuts would be appreciated, but if necessary, steal it, because these guys (birds) were adept at swiping a nut and flying away quicker than I could react. So I was an easy target and gave him a peanut, shell and all. As he chattered and flew away, I wasn't sure whether he was expressing gratitude or swearing at me. The raucous notes sounded more like the latter.

Soon he was back, chattering like mad, which I thought meant, "Get a deer, clean it out, I want to get my pick of the intestines before the other animals do." To which I muttered some conciliatory kindness.

Better to feed the jays than to get a Boone & Crockett rack? No, but the option wasn't quite that simple.

Heck, no. The game was deer hunting, not bird feeding. At the end of the day, enjoying a brandy with my fellow hunters, they would boo me out of the shack if I told them that all I did was feed the jacks, whose only role in life seemed to be cadging food.

So leave the peanuts in the pocket and be alert for a deer.

WILLIAM HULL
Edina, MN 55435

I Wouldn't Kill Bambi

Those of us who are hunters have many reasons for following this particular activity, a sport in itself, although we realize there are some people who do not share our enthusiasm. We respect their opinions, even when we suspect they do not respect ours. This is an attempt to respond to the woman who telephoned me when she heard I was collecting material for this book, cursed at me, and said, "I hope your book goes down the toilet."

Men and women hunt for many reasons; here are a few of them.

1. To supply food for the family. Every single hunter I have ever met consumes the meat from a downed deer. It is delicious, nutritive meat and can be used in many different recipes. Hunters' families enjoy venison roasts, chops, steaks, ground venisonburgers, sausages, sausages mixed with pork as an extender, stew, many, many delicious dishes.

The reaction to success by a hunter varies widely. I've seen grown men cry when they achieved the goal and downed a deer. I've seen them vomit when they had to clean out their downed animal. I've seen them exult at their personal achievement, but, I've never seen or heard them brag about the kill for the kill's sake. There's nothing satisfying about shooting a deer, whether by arrow, shotgun slug, or rifle lead. It's a necessary act to make the meat available and clean. The aesthetics disturb a lot of people. It's not too distant from the early man who had to dress out a huge water buffalo, a deep sea whale, or even a prairie buffalo. It's simply not pleasurable.

2. To perpetuate early mankind's organized hunt. Even after man learned to domesticate some animals and to breed and raise them for food purposes, man still went on organized hunts in the jungles and on the plains to obtain additional food, or food that tantalized their taste buds differently, the rituals of becoming a man—the hunt in which he was privileged to participate only when he was accepted as being worthy, with proper endurance for the activity, of being one of the man clan. It was a great honor to be so recognized, and worthy of joining the hunt . . .

3. . . . . which leads to the sheer joy of being together in a group

19

of men friends for a weekend. To this writer I suspect that the
sheer camaraderie of being with friends on a weekend hunt is a
major part of the appeal. To joke with others, to rehash previous
successes and failures, to rough it by sleeping in a sleeping bag,
on hard boards, in a shack so beaten up their spouses wouldn't
believe it—to show the world that they can cook edible food
over a rusty wood stove that has no temperature controls like the
stove at home, to plan and provide for rations to satisfy ravenous
appetites. It's usually not a drinking weekend, as some critics
claim, because true hunters insist that each member be cold
sober and without aftereffects of drinking when they take their
death stick into the woods. Observe a group of men gathered together at one man's house to watch a weekend football game.
Project this into a rural shack where the temperature is near zero
outside and not a lot better inside. There's a strong similarity in
both situations.

4. To test oneself. Boys go through self-administered tests regardless of age. Early in life they want to prove their ability, their
strength, their honor by being the best. The best, the leader, at
snowball fights, at running games, at swimming in the swimming hole or pool, their general derring-do. From early age they
seem to know that as adults they are going to need certain
strengths and abilities to fight the challenges of adult life. It is
fun for a boy to be the leader of a small neighborhood gang, or
even to be a part of the gang. It is fun for a grown man to joke
with the sleepy-head they practically have to pull out of bed in
the shack at 3:30 A.M. to go deer hunting. Again, it is a challenge
and men like challenges. To some, that is the very existence of
their adult life; many prefer challenges; they sometimes seek em-
ployment with challenges versus the sure thing of a soft work-
place. So, never underestimate the element of fun of being in the
hunting party. That element far overshadows the thrill of the
hunt, the kill. Thus, when hunting, he may be asking himself,
"Do I have the fortitude to put up with great discomfort, miserable sleeping conditions, plenty of inexpensive food? What are
my personal limits of strength and determination?"

5. To control the deer population, which in some areas has
gotten out of control. In many county parks deer have become

so numerous that they stray into farmers' fields and destroy such large quantities of crops that they have become a nuisance. State departments of natural resources or state game warden groups quite frequently provide controlled hunting in such parks, emphasizing that the herd must be reduced so the remaining animals can be stronger and bear stronger young. The land can support only a certain number of wild animals, providing food and water, and if we permit the animals per acre to exceed that level, DNR people say we can expect starvation and disease, so they frequently encourage deer hunting seasons.

6. To prove, again, his manliness to his spouse and children. Daddy lived in a miserable shack over the weekend, sleeping on a plain board bunk, had no opportunity for a bath, couldn't shave because there was no hot water, or no tree hit by lightning into which to plug his electric shaver. All of this leads to him being placed closer to the pedestal of admiration by spouse and kids. "My daddy got his deer. He's a real man."

7. The creation of Bambi has done lots to harm the picture of the hunter. However, if the people who say, "You wouldn't kill Bambi would you?" could see what can happen to Bambi if left in an overcrowded forest, if they could see the starvation, the dead deer lying along the roadside, they might not be quite so critical. They shouldn't be that way, for many reasons, particularly as they use an extra sharp steak knife to cut their filet mignon, taken from a prime piece of beef. Someone killed it, maybe with a blow to the head or maybe with a gunshot on the slaughterhouse line.

WILLIAM H. HULL
Edina, Minnesota

Grabbed the Deer By the Tail and Off They Went

This hunt took place fifty years ago in Beardsley, Minnesota, at Bonanza beach. It was the first deer season in Big Stone County.

The hunting party consisted of two of my uncles, Jim Davidson and George Haanen, my dad, Jack Haanen, and my grandfather, Jim Davidson.

There were no shotgun slugs available, so Jim reloaded steel ball bearings into some shells for slugs.

On the day before the season, their licenses hadn't come in the mail, but they still went hunting. The next morning George came back to town to get the licenses from the post office and stopped by to tell us they had two deer. I wasn't hunting yet but went back with him to see the deer. When we got to the top of the hill, he borrowed three shells from my grandfather because his were all gone. As we were walking down the hill, I was on the outside on this old road and I could see two deer on the bluff above the road. I whispered to George to move over by me. He saw them and fired three shots, knocking one down. He ran up there and about that time the deer got up. George dropped his gun and grabbed the deer by the tail and down through the woods they went. George was so out of wind I could hear him moaning, but he wouldn't let go. Finally they reached Jim who yelled at George to let go so he could shoot the deer—and that's the way it was.

Those ball bearings that he was shooting went pretty straight, but there was no expansion with them; they sure whistled when they left a gun barrel. I think the whistle was caused by the steel-on-steel effect. I know they weren't too large because he dropped them down the barrel of a full choke to be sure they wouldn't split the barrel when they came out.

Lou Haanen
Beardsley, Minnesota

A Massive Deer

I want to start this yarn with, "It was in and about the Martinmas time and the green leaves were a-fallin'"[1] but that really isn't pertinent because the green leaves had already fallen long ago and now were covered with a foot of snow.

Yes, we were deer hunting out of a gyppo shack up north at Cook; it was our first night of the hunting season and we were gathering back at the shack after a day of cold work. None of us had even seen a deer, until Bob came in—the last to check in for the day—and quickly told us of his good news. He had bagged the biggest doe he had ever seen and needed help to quarter it and bring the pieces back to camp. As proof, he had brought along the liver which we could cook for dinner. Having just come off a heart attack, I was pardoned from the heavy work and left at the shack while the others went to fetch hunks of this giant doe.

I had the dubious privilege of staying in camp to fry the liver, which had to be done practically in the dark because the one kerosene lamp didn't offer much light. So the other guys re-dressed and took off, leaving me to do my part.

Of course, the big iron barrel, which had been made into a stove with a flat steel surface welded atop as a cooking surface, would provide plenty of heat from the burning popple inside. I am a pretty good cook, but that night I wasn't proud of my achievements. When the guys came back, each carrying a quarter of that doe, with cold wet hands from performing field surgery on the animal, they were a hungry mob, but not hungry for my hard, overcooked, nearly burnt liver.

Words were exchanged. None kindly. Bob was most vociferous of all. Liver steaks went flying out the door to sizzle in the deep snow. The heat wasn't solely in that red hot stove. Damn! There were a few sad moments.

Whatever we ate that night, it was sufficient, because we always took plenty of alternate food along on those trips.

Reminds me of the great meals we had at my grandparent Hull's house when I was a kid. At every possible occasion, whether it was a national holiday, someone's birthday or an anniversary, we gathered at my grandparents' house to celebrate the event. When my dad's five siblings, their spouses, and kids gathered, and perhaps Uncle Neil (Grandad's bachelor older brother) there were nearly twenty-five of us. It took a lot of food to feed that hungry clan, even more so if Grandad had made some of his famous (or infamous) country eggnog with Old Grandad himself and lots of fresh cream and eggs.

The meal was a noontime affair, with one of those huge, groaning kitchen tables people talk about. Not only did every family bring food to contribute, but Grandmother Hull had turkey, maybe roast beef, and pies galore. We ate well, stuffing ourselves.

After dinner, those older folks who could find a cozy chair and who could ignore the noise of the kids, would fall asleep or play cards, until the shadows became long and the end of the day approached. The sign of that happening was the lighting of the first coal-oil (kerosene) lamp.

About then a kid or two would sneak into the kitchen to find a fried chicken leg or a piece of fruit pie; my choice was universally known as being gooseberry.

Some adult would be sure to see us swiping food.

"Now, George Henry, get out of that chicken. Didn't you eat enough at dinnertime?"

"Billy! Are you eating another piece of pie? How can you eat so much?"

You understand. This was just good-natured banter. Just kidding. Because in minutes, maybe seconds, one or two adults would join us in looking for something more to eat.

Then Aunt Gladys would come in.

"You men and kids!" she'd exclaim. "How can we ever fill you up?" And she'd shrug her shoulders at the impossibility of keeping us food satisfied.

Then she'd lead the table-refilling crew. "Just hold your horses and we'll put out what's left over."

And out would come more heaps of food.

Aunt Geneva would say, "Shall I cut up the rest of this ham? Wonder if they'll eat it cold or should I warm up slices in a skillet?"

Aunt Flora would volunteer to peel a big panful of apples and quickly stew them with some brown sugar in another skillet.

Someone would find a large piece of beef roast still in good shape; another would round up all the leftover pieces of pies, plus an occasional whole one, perhaps even a raisin.

Grandmother would start another big pot of coffee in her blue porcelain pot, and about that time Uncle John would say, "Well, hurry it up, girls. It's getting dark and I have to get home to feed."

So with all the contributions we'd sit down to a second huge meal. Maybe even homemade bread or Aunt Geneva's glorious biscuits. We ate it all and appreciated it, too.

On one occasion Uncle Pat said, "I'll go to town to get some ice and we can make ice cream." Why not? There was always plenty of fresh cream and milk and eggs galore, so that would become a glorious extra dessert.

We ate well and quickly. We kids stayed our ground and no one could push us aside to a children's table, so we sat around that huge kitchen table and ate another fine meal, in some ways the best of the day, but still memorable. I'm sure I'm not the only one to remember those second meals more than a half century later.

BILL HULL

1. From the song "Barbara Allen".

A Little Girl Has a Dream

All of us have dreams, but in a lifetime few of us have them come true. It all began back in November 1934, when I was a little girl only three-and-one-half years old; I was a tomboy because I had a baby sister (Betty) who was six months old. So I became daddy's little girl.

This was the first time in many years that there was a Wisconsin open gun season for deer. My story began early one spring morning when my father, Oscar D. Dang, was in the barbershop to get his hair cut. Where else could you get the latest information about what was going on in town? They were all talking about the upcoming deer season in the fall. No one knew what it was all about or where to go. The first problem was that they were all in Franklin County and there was to be no open season in that county. The nearest was in the adjoining Gasconda County.

One thing led to another and the barber asked my father to go with him, but my father didn't have a gun, so he borrowed one from a friend even though the season wouldn't open until the following November.

All summer long father was given lots of advice from all the would-be hunters, but before they realized it, November had come.

Soon the actual day was here. Mother woke my father at 4:00 A.M., although she'd had very little sleep due to worrying about him going hunting. She raced to the kitchen to prepare him breakfast and to pack him a lunch.

It was cold—long john weather. After getting ready, my father kissed mother and us kids good-bye and told us not to worry. He was in a hurry. We lived just one mile from the little town of Gerald, population 309, where he had to pick up his partner, the barber. Then they would have to drive another twenty miles to get to the place where they had permission to hunt. Then they were to walk about 500 yards to go to their individual hunting stands in the woods.

At home, mother kept herself busy feeding the animals. She had to do it all that morning because father had to leave so early.

As a livestock dealer, he always had new animals around. Mother had cared for them and had returned to the house by the time my sister and I woke up. Then she fixed our breakfasts.

Soon the telephone rang. We were on a party line so everybody knew what was happening. Mother had my little sister in her arms when she answered the telephone. She immediately began to cry, worried that something had happened to my father. The call was early, only 9 A.M.

He was just calling from town to tell her he was okay, that he was back in town, and that he had killed a seven-point buck.

Before they went hunting, the two men had agreed that the successful hunter would get the rack and skin and half the meat, the other half of the meat going to his partner.

After Daddy came home, the news got around that he had killed the deer. I remember that people came from all around to see the deer and to get just a small amount of meat. After it was all over, there was very little left for our family.

When I was older and out of school, I always wanted to go hunting, but during all those years my parents wouldn't let me go. Then, when I was out of school I got a job with Uncle Sam and was sent to Washington, D.C. From there I was lucky and was transferred to St. Louis, just fifty miles from home, my parents having moved to Union, Missouri. I saved my vacation so I could go on my dream hunt for deer.

The last week of work was all talk about me, a woman, going deer hunting. So, when Friday finally came, I left right after work, having only an hour's drive. Mother, a great cook, had supper ready and we pitched right in. After supper my father and I began to get everything ready for the next day, the first day of the gun deer season; it was November 1952.

We only had to go a few miles out of town from where my parents live in Union. So, before we knew it, mother was calling, "It's time to get up now; you said to awaken you at 4 A.M. —so rise and shine! Breakfast will be ready in just as few minutes." Then she added, "Be sure to dress warmly. Its twenty degrees out there."

It wasn't long before mother had her great breakfast ready—

orange juice, oatmeal, eggs, ham, biscuits, apple butter and coffee—a good way to begin the day. She'd also packed us lunches.

On the previous day, my father had been to the farm where
we were to hunt, doing some business with the farmer who had
told him the deer would be back the following day. He said that
that very morning the deer had crossed the hay field to go to the
north woods and they'd probably repeat that today. He also gave
my father permission to return the next day and assured Dad
that the deer would be back.

We left home all set for a day of hunting and hoping the
farmer knew what he was talking about. We arrived at the farm
an hour before sunrise, getting to the stand only took about
thirty minutes.

We got behind some cedar trees at the edge of the field where
the deer were to pass. This being my first deer hunt, I stayed with
my father.

Shortly after sunrise we heard noises from the brush at our far
left. As we turned to look in that direction, here came the deer, a
beautiful four-point buck and two does. As they gathered in
front of us at about one hundred yards, my father said, "You take
the front one and I'll take the second, the buck. Shoot." His deer
dropped in his tracks, but mine ran to the fence row and just
stopped there. I tried to shoot again, but I couldn't. My gun
jammed. I told my father to shoot my deer, that I couldn't. He
said, "No. You got him. His tail has dropped. He can't go on,"
while here I am having a heart attack. "Go check my deer and I'll
take care of yours," I said. He was right because my deer fell over
dead before he got to him. When I reached my father's deer, I
had quite a surprise. I had thought he downed a larger animal,
but his deer had one antler with four points while the other
antler only had two points, half was broken off. There was a
snare wrapped around the two remaining points. Was he surprised when he came to see his deer.

This was the beginning of a lifelong hunter partnership with
my father. This was only our first year. Our luck changed. We
killed deer but not both on the first day of the season. We hunted
together and with others until my dad went to the happy hunting ground at the age of eighty-four years.

After getting married late in life (1972) and retiring from my government job, my husband joined us in our deer hunting. We all had great times and I had two great partners, but I guess it's time to quit because I missed last year.

Leave it to the young hunters. But I love being in the woods.

Shirley Wilmesher
Union, Missouri

The Chase

I worked at the store on Saturday, December 4, 1993, all morning and then met a group of guys at the Tom Thumb at Dassel at about 1 P.M. The group included Chuck Schoolmeesters, Chuck, Steve and Jason Schultz, Dave Sonsalla and his two boys, Nick and Eric, as well as Roger Arens. We headed for a large unpicked cornfield about a mile southeast of Dassel. Snow was a few inches deep. I was a bowhunter.

I was chosen to take a stand in the woods at the edge of a field. It was after a long wait I saw four does break from the corn to the west of me and head toward Steve Schultz, who was behind me.

Another twenty minutes passed and I saw one of the drivers coming through the corn ahead of me. Then a buck appeared on the next hill behind him headed west through the corn. I could not tell how big it was, but it appeared to be limping as it crashed through the corn. I came out to the edge of the corn and saw a six-point buck break out and head east toward the other guys on stands. I was curious about the deer, which appeared to be limping, and went to see his track. I found the first track and followed it out of the corn and determined that he was running on three legs.

I followed him down a steep hill through woods and west toward the road. He went through an abandoned farm site and veered around the trucks of the guys who made the drive.

He then crossed the road and went through a fence and into a low swampy area, then up over a brushy hill and across a winter wheat field. After crossing the forty acres of wheat, heading south, he slowed to a walk and headed east along a fence line, then crossed the line into a plowed field heading southwest again. After several hundred yards, he came to a dip in the rolling hills of the plowed field. He was a hundred yards ahead of me and running straight south. He disappeared over the next hill and I ran after him.

I came to the top of the hill and was surprised to see nothing ahead of me except a small woods a quarter of a mile away. I stood panting and finally caught a glimpse of movement in the woods heading to my left. I marked the spot and headed for those woods.

It was difficult to find his track again because the woods were full of deer tracks. I backtracked to the edge of the woods and found where he had entered, judging by the size and direction of his tracks. He headed out of the woods along a fence line full of brush and was now headed straight east.

He came up onto the tar road and followed it south a short ways, then crossed and headed east across another plowed forty-acre field. I stood on the tar road and looked east toward the woods for which he headed. Suddenly he appeared, jumped a fence, and disappeared into the woods. Again I marked the spot and headed across the field. Slowly I followed his tracks as I traveled through a thick, low area riddled with fallen logs.

He came out of the woods and followed a line of trees along the edge of a wheat-stubble field. I followed as he continued east, and as I neared the end of the field, he broke away in front of me. I tried to stay hidden as he entered a brushy area that went around a small lake. I watched as he went around the south end of the lake and then turned north again. I circled around and came out on a road that was above his route—following the road that went around the lake and down a steep bank ahead of where I had last seen him. There was his trail again. He continued north across a small field and into some brush. As I came through the brush I saw a pickup on the gravel road to the east. They hit the brakes and drove onto a Conservation Reserve Program (CRP) field, pointing at something. I guessed they were seeing the buck, so I took off in their direction. I finally caught up with them, and they said he had crossed the railroad tracks and was just over the edge of a bank that went down to Highway 12. I eased over and didn't see him, but on looking across the road I saw him a quarter of a mile ahead. He had crossed back over the highway and was headed north across another CRP field. I dropped down and waited for a chance to cross the road.

Two boys in a small blue car yelled that they had seen him cross the road. I picked up his track again and followed him across the CRP field. When he would go out of sight into a low spot, I would move up as far as I could and then wait, hiding behind any available weeds and grass. As he neared the end of the CRP field he stopped and stared in every direction, while I watched him through my binoculars. Finally, satisfied that he was not being followed, he walked out of sight amongst some brush. I ran up to peer over the hill and saw him about fifty yards ahead as he turned and headed into the brush.

I waited a few minutes to catch my breath, then swung out into the field so my scent wouldn't carry to him. As I slowly approached the cover, he broke out and I took a quick twenty-yard shot as he quickly quartered away. He ran about forty yards with me chasing, then slowed with my arrow angling from his stomach into his chest area. He slowed to a walk and stopped by the roadside. At fifteen yards I put a second arrow behind his front leg.

For a second he just looked at me as I knelt in the snow; then he turned and trotted toward me before falling at about five yards before reaching me.

I would like to report that I stood my ground, but I was up and running the other way. In a moment his head dropped and it was all over. The chase had taken two and a half hours and covered about five miles.

I admired his rack for a while and then started to gut him. The two boys in the blue car had followed and came running across the field from where they parked. They helped me gut the deer and then gave me a ride back to my truck, where I wrote the other hunters a note telling where I was headed and waited there at a friend's house. Soon they all arrived and we dragged the deer to our cars.

His even ten-point rack scored about 130, my largest to date.

His back leg was broken just below the hock where there is no muscle, probably shot or hit by a car. He had lost weight but still was a beautiful animal. On his three legs he could still outrun me easily.

I will have his head mounted, not as a trophy of my ability, but rather as a tribute and respect for this magnificent animal that I had the privilege to hunt.

BRENT SWANSON
Dassell, Minnesota

May I Watch You Dress Out That Deer?

Yes, that's what the voice suddenly asked from directly behind me.

"May I watch you dress out that deer? I've never seen it done and don't know how when I get my deer."

Of course I consented, but was surprised to find him right behind me when there was not supposed to be anyone else in my assigned area.

This was an unusual situation for me. Probably in the fall of 1981, but anyhow, a few years ago, I had gone through a serious heart attack which had originated with a bad accident and soon a case of congestive heart failure developed. I was familiar with that problem because that was what had killed my maternal grandfather before I was even born. Only then they called it "dropsy."

As a result, I had to forgo the usual Up North hunting trip in early November, but not wanting to be left out of the season completely had applied for a raffled chance to hunt in a county park, where an excess number of deer needed to be thinned out to avoid complete destruction of nearby farm crops, mainly corn. This culling was to be at Carver County Park, which is about twenty-five miles west of where I live in suburban Minneapolis. It is a beautiful park, complete with a nature center building, many hiking trails, and apparently lots of deer. This was to be an any-sex hunt to make it all the more attractive, and it was to be a shotgun-only hunt, partly, if not mainly, for safety's sake. After all, there were residential areas adjoining this large park and there could be no chance of high caliber slugs ripping into the nearby houses.

So, my name was called and I reported to the planning meeting of the lucky guys and gals. There, in rotation, we were given a chance to request a preferred hunting area or, if not, to be assigned one. I had my choice and was assigned a spot off a secondary road about a hundred yards in, where I had an opportunity to select a stand to my liking, since the actual hunting dates were ten to twenty days away. (I have forgotten the actual span.)

I had selected a spot near the top of a grade, where I could sit

on the ground, with my back against a good-sized tree, with an
old barn at least fifty yards behind me. I overlooked a gentle
slope leading down to a scattering of trees, a very small creek,
now frozen over, and a rising cornfield beyond that. To my right
was an open area leading to a cornfield at the top of a slope, with
the land tapering down to that little clump of sparse trees; I was
thinking that the night-feeding deer might congregate amongst
those trees to settle for the day, or perhaps they would come
there hoping to find some water in the little creek.

So, I arose early to be in position by sunup, did all the necessary preparatory work, drove the twenty-five miles in my full-
sized van, parked it off the road near the barn, and took my
stand, warmed with a cup of hot coffee and eating a bun or roll.
Now, deer, come on.

Oh, I thought, I've never shot, or even shot at, large game
with anything but a rifle. How high do I aim to hit a deer? What
will be the trajectory of my twelve-gauge slug? How damned
cold is it anyway?

Hunters, you know how it goes! Wait, wait, wait. Is that
movement? Did I hear a twig break? That must be a deer, but
where is it? It's still not completely light and is very hard to see.
Bah! That's just your imagination. Have another sandwich. So I
did.

Then, there is movement. There they are! A doe and two yearlings. They're directly below me in the clump of trees. Quickly I
took aim at one of those tender-looking young yearlings, raised
my sights to provide for the drop due to that great distance, and
squeezed the trigger.

WHAM! Boy, a shotgun is noisy on a still winter morning.
Like a real novice I jumped to my feet to see if I had hit the yearling. But no. I had aimed too high, clipped off a branch over the
youngster's head, and had not even disturbed them. Even the
noise hadn't affected them. They hadn't even moved.

What to do? Hell, go for the doe.

So I put another shell in the chamber, aimed less high, and
put that doe down and out with a perfect shot. This time I was
still standing and could see her go down. I had my deer! I went
down that slope in record time while the yearlings took off at top

speed. No need to worry about them. They were long ago weened and could care for themselves now.

There she was. A young doe—probably the yearlings were her first offspring—in apparently good condition, pleasantly fat but not heavy. I started to dress her, thinking about that long pull up the hill to get her into the van to go home; but first things first, with my trusty sheath knife, I started eviscerating the animal, to let it bleed out (better for the meat) and to reduce the weight I'd have to move to the van.

That's when I heard that voice directly behind me, a startling situation because I had just had the adrenaline-raising experience of the kill.

"May I watch you dress out that deer? I've never seen it done before." Of course I consented, actually suggesting that he could help keep the legs out of the way while I continued cleaning up the carcass. All the time I was thinking that this young man needed a father. How come he didn't have a dad to go with him and to pass on some knowledge and skill? But that was none of my business.

We were about through when he suddenly turned and said, "Well, thank you. I've got to get going," and before I could speak up, he was gone.

While I stood there, amazed that I had let him go, not pointing out to him that I needed his help to pull that big doe up the hill through all the frozen farm brush and to load it into the van.

But, too late. He was gone.

So I did it myself. Rope around the animal, pulling it up, getting stuck on saplings and thornbushes, panting like mad, sweat popping out all over me, thinking, Am I in danger? No, I told myself. Just take it easy. So easy to say, "Take it easy."

Finally I was at the van, keys in the pocket, opening the rear cargo doors, looking at that carcass which now seemed huge. Trying to pick it up while it was so relaxed. Each effort to get it into the van resulted in the animal dropping back to the ground, cursing myself for not asking the young man for help, then blaming him for being so calloused. Oh, yes, he knew I was recovering, but I hadn't said, "Hey, Jim, will you help me get this monster up the hill and inside the van? That's going to be too tough for one guy to handle." Of couse he would have helped.

Anyway, it was a successful hunt and I had a good doe. We'd have venison meat in the locker again.

Bill Hull

Five Hunters, Five Shots, Five Deer, Five Days

I've been a logger for fifty years and have seen a lot of things in the woods.

One day as I was driving along a country road I saw a small, newly born fawn by the side of the road. I didn't want to stop right on the curve of the road so drove around the corner, stopped, and walked back to where I had just seen the fawn. I couldn't see that little deer any place, even in the ditch along the road. Then I saw a lily pad move. It was that little thing hiding with its nose lifting that lily pad so it could breathe.

At another time my brother-in-law and I were walking in a cedar swamp. There wasn't much snow but just enough that we noticed there were cedar branches dropped along the way. Then we noticed a porcupine up in a cedar tree cutting branches for the deer to eat. We knew they were doing it for that purpose because porkies don't eat cedar; they go into birch trees to feed on the bark, not cedars.

But the story I really want to tell you is about something that happened twenty or twenty-five years ago.

There were five hunters in our deer-hunting party.

My brother-in-law was on a stand one cold and snowy day. As he was walking back to the hunting shack he saw a nice deer in a swamp. He shot it and got it with one shot.

The next day a friend of his from southern Minnesota was sneak hunting in some hilly country about two miles from our shack. As he was tracking a deer in the snow, he went around a hill and met a six-point buck in the trail, which he quickly shot, and got a second deer with one shot.

That brought us to two deer, for two shots.

On the third day another one of our party heard two bucks fighting in the balsam bushes; he waited until one of the bucks ran out from the fight and he got it—that was three shots, three deer.

On the fourth day another one of our party was tracking and the deer went into a small spruce swamp. He walked around the swamp and waited for the deer to come out. Then he noticed that it had come out already. He did that a couple of times and then saw the deer running on a hillside—and shot it. Again with one shot.

We thought this was getting unbelievable, four for four!

Now I was the only one who hadn't bagged a deer so the pressure was on me. I was walking along a fence line and saw a forked buck running toward the fence; so I aimed my rifle on the fence, I pulled the trigger, and the deer landed on the other side, so that made it five hunters, five deer, five shots, five days.

We called it a very successful hunt.

JONAS HEIKKILA
Wright, Minnesota

Up Went the Ducks and Down Came the Bucks

Whitetail deer hunting is a tradition which has been in our family for the past four generations in eastern Ottertail County, Minnesota.

The excitement of friends and family coming together for the weekend hunt, the stories told and retold, and the harvest of those beautiful corn-fed whitetails, makes for a wonderful weekend for each of us.

The DNR talks about the quality hunt. Well, I know we've had that in our family for many years.

My younger brother and I had gone through the early morning stand hunt and hadn't seen a deer. Our party had harvested two bucks and three does on Swede's Hill, as we found out while having our morning lunch.

So we decided to walk around or perhaps to drive.

When we had reached the east side of the farmyard overlooking a large willows-cattail slough, we had but one small slough to push before rejoining our hunting party.

Mark was to the right and, since I shoot left-handed, I was on his far left, some thirty yards away. We had a small board fence to cross before we could push the small cattail slough. Mark had crossed the old fence and was just closing his bolt on the 30-06 when apparently the movement of the fence caused it to collapse.

As it collapsed, the noise startled some fifteen to twenty mallards that were resting in the old pond just yards away. Suddenly the tall grass between us and the pond came alive with antlers and massive brown bodies. One of the deer bolted to the right, and fortunately for me, the larger of the two ran to the left. When calm was restored, Mark had a nice seven-pointer and I had a very nice eight-pointer to add to the old windmill meat pole back on Dad's dairy farm.

Years later, Dad still enjoys hearing the story of "The Ducks Got Up and the Bucks Went Down."

Each year the neighbors, friends and people from other hunting parties call to see how the Hemquist party did. We've been so fortunate to have ample land, good crops, excellent breeding animals, and excellent stewardship as demonstrated by my father, Carroll Hemquist. We always harvest eleven, twelve, thirteen deer with twelve to fifteen hunters. Now, with the addition of sons, nephews, and other friends, we have added a 100-acre parcel, a 120-acre parcel and another of 160 acres to Dad's 365-acre farm, a total of nearly 750 acres, ensuring habitat for future hunting seasons.

Good hunting.

HARRIS W. HEMQUIST
Baxter, Minnesota

Passing on the Sport

For three generations the Gau family's annual deer hunt has been a tradition of father and son togetherness. I accompanied my father and grandfather for my first experience at deer hunting in 1965 at the age of nine. (I didn't get to carry a gun until several years later.) I remember going into the woods with my grandfather and sitting with him in a big platform, which the hunters called "the porcupine stand." We didn't see any deer that time.

We hunt near a town called Togo in northern Minnesota, northeast of Grand Rapids. My grandfather and a group of seven other men started hunting there in 1939, and my father started there in 1946. Originally they pitched a large sixteen-foot-by-sixteen-foot tent for the camp. The tent had a wood-burning stove for heat, a dirt floor, and a large cot, which went across the entire tent where all eight men slept. The camp was moved several times in 1962, when the hunting cabin we are presently using was built. The conveniences aren't much better; we still have wood heat, no running water, and an outdoor toilet, but it is much warmer and roomier and has a gas stove and gas lights.

The number of hunters varies from year to year, depending on whether someone has passed away or dropped out of the group, but there is room for eight. My grandfather, by the way, died ten years ago. I then inherited his share of the camp.

The hunt begins by setting up the camp. Windows are uncovered, the floor is swept, dishes are washed, and food and gear are put in their proper places. After dinner, hunting strategies are discussed and planned. After the planning, many stories and tales of past hunts are exchanged. Bedtime comes early in anticipation of the day's hunt. Morning comes even earlier (unless we feel like sleeping some more) with a light breakfast, and then it's out to the deer stands. Time goes slowly, and every strange sound puts you on guard for the chance of seeing a deer. Sometimes the waiting pays off. Hopefully, after several days of hunting, the group will have something to show for its efforts. If not, we're always thankful for a safe hunt and the time we had together. I know that for me, being able to spend time with my father and friends is the most important part of the hunt.

LARRY GAU
Dayton, Minnesota.

Stan the Man, a Folding Chair, and a Buck in Rut

The 1992 Minnesota rifle season for deer was also the thirtieth anniversary of our group's hunting shack. Located thirty miles south of the Canadian border on a paper company lease site, "shack" is the accurate description. "Cabin" is not the accurate description. When the basic description is reassembled sections of an old wood-constructed garage, with open rafters and mismatched exterior siding, we are definitely talking "shack." A "cabin," in our group's opinion, is a higher-class structure, with perhaps a normal ceiling and substantial insulation throughout.

However, our affection for our shack could not be greater if it indeed were a cabin. Comfortable evenings, complete with the requisite retelling of numerous deer stories while seated around the wood-burning stove, continually adds to the fellowship of our remaining trio of members. In our group's heyday thirty years ago, eight to ten people populated the shack during hunting season.

The senior man in our trio is my father, Stan the Man Olson. He is truly The Man because of his patience and creative expertise to build or fix almost anything.

We transported our shack sections and building materials through severe swamp thickets with homemade wheeled and tracked vehicles that Stan built in the fifties and sixties—years before the advent of snowmobiles and ATVs. I have continually challenged this expert welder and mechanic to fabricate my own gadget ideas.

One of the best collaborations we developed is a four-inch diameter pocket mirror with a screw-in T-anchor that mounts on any size tree, including saplings as small as your thumb. Each of us carries one and uses it when still hunting on area logging roads or trails. You can remain motionless while facing one direction and still see the road behind. Much success in seeing and bagging deer for our camp can be attributed to these pocket mirrors.

In 1992 another item of equipment made it onto the success list—a folding chair. A rental firm was discarding several bent and broken folding chairs which featured steel tubing construction with orange plastic seats and backrests. Unhesitatingly, I hauled them home to Stan the Man for weld repair and reinforcement. The plan would be to use them at select hunting locations in our area during the upcoming season.

On opening day Stan still-hunted a couple of customary spots until noon, without success. After lunch at the shack he decided to monitor a stretch of logging road that heads east of the shack. It is only a quarter mile walk to that stretch so Stan carried one of the repaired folding chairs with him and still hunted there until 4 P.M. The two-inch deep cover of snow on the ground would offer a great contrasting backdrop for any deer that might appear.

It was after 4 P.M. and he was returning westbound on the east-west logging road that traverses our shack. He was wearing his loose-fitting blaze orange-billed cap, carrying the folding chair he grabbed after lunch, and had his 30-06 scoped automatic rifle slung on his shoulder. The sky was overcast, which is common to much of Minnesota in November.

There is a curve in the logging road, which denotes the access road to our shack. As Stan rounded this bend, in front of our shack, his eyes focused on the westbound stretch.

There it was! A mature eight-point buck standing in the center of the road, 240 yards away. What a majestic picture. The buck's head was erect, staring back at Stan, and his entire body was framed with a backdrop of white snow. Now that is a sight to accelerate the heartbeat of any hunter, especially Stan's, who had not bagged a deer during the five previous seasons.

The buck stood motionless.

What happened next confirms the fact that this buck was in a rutting stupor and had only one thing on his mind.

Because of the distance (240 yards) and his lack of confidence in his offhand steadiness as a 72-year-old man, Stan opened the folding chair he was carrying and knelt behind it to use the backrest as a steadying rest for his rifle.

The buck stayed motionless.

Stan positioned his rifle on the chair's backrest in the palm of the buckskin chopper on his left hand. The buck still remained rigid.

Stan pressed the rifle stock against his shoulder and looked for the crosshairs in the scope. The only problem was that the bill of his loose-fitting cap slid forward and obscured his vision. He reached up with his right hand and rotated the cap 180 degrees until the bill of the cap pointed backwards on his head, the rally-cap position popularized by the youth of the nineties. The buck, fortunately, still had not moved.

Stan steadied the crosshairs on the heart/lung cavity and squeezed the trigger.

I was still-hunting one-half mile to the west. Upon hearing the "thwook-bang" of the solitary shot, I immediately packed my gear and headed toward our shack.

The tracks in the snow confirmed my suspicions. Dad was just beginning to field dress the 190-pound eight-pointer when I arrived. The buck had gone only thirty yards before succumbing to the well-placed heart shot. High fives between Dad and me were exchanged and the details of his encounter with the folding-chair buck were relayed before we completed the field dressing job.

A few years ago we started a tradition in the camp of toasting each hunter who bags a whitetail. The toast involves a straight shot of Yukon Jack, a Canadian liquor which takes your breath away, much like certain moments one experiences while deer hunting. Because this buck ended a five-year drought for Stan, the three of us had our breath taken away more than once that evening!

Nineteen ninety-two was truly a special anniversary year for our camp, but it will be remembered forever for that opening day when Stan the Man used a folding chair to nail a buck in rut.

LEN OLSON
Minneapolis, Minnesota

It's NOT Just "Getting a Deer"

As I peeked down the corn row, I saw a brown form about forty yards down the row. This is what we had come into the cornfield looking for. I pulled my head back out of the corn row and quietly motioned for my partner to take a look. He stuck his head through the row and observed the deer for a few minutes, then pulled his head back from the row and eagerly gave me the thumbs-up signal. I could see by the excitement in his eyes, it was time to make our move.

My partner was my son, Jason. Although he had just had his seventh birthday, he had been my loyal sidekick throughout the bow season. I had not bowhunted for several years and, partly due to Jason's interest in the outdoors, I decided to get back into it. He took an immediate interest in bowhunting. He watched me practice during the summer. His cousin Justin, gave him a nine-pound recurve so he could practice with me. As the season approached we spent several evenings scouting different areas and planning our strategies. He helped select our stands and clear shooting lanes. He practiced with the grunt call and rattled with the set of horns we put together. He became aware of the whitetail's world.

Once the season began we agreed that a portable stand was not big enough for the two of us so he would not be able to hunt with me when the stand was used. To keep him involved we did get out frequently and used the larger, more comfortable rifle stands. These were excellent observation nights. One evening we used a different scent to attract the wily whitetail. Jason pulled a sack of barbecued potato chips out of his pocket and began munching. We thought maybe a nice buck would like the smell and wander by. Nothing that night!

When mid-November rolled around we had an unusual situation in Minnesota. The corn crop was late and the snow was early. The deer were spending a lot of time eating corn so we decided to stalk them in the field.

When we woke up Saturday morning conditions seemed ideal—a couple of inches of new snow, temperatures in the twenties for quiet walking, and an adequate northwest wind to mask the noise in the cornfield and to carry our scent in the right direction. We jumped into our pickup and headed to our land thirty miles away. When we arrived we were surprised to find eighteen inches of new snow. We stopped at my mother's house to have a glass of milk, a cup of coffee, and to reconsider our plan. It would be tough walking for Jason in that much snow, but he was determined to give it a try.

With my bow in hand and my seven-year-old sidekick right beside me, we headed out Mom's back door, through the woods, and to the cornfield. It was an incredible day.

Throughout the fall we had taken time to notice the magic of the forest—the beauty of the trees, the special calls of the birds, the freshness of the air, and the feeling of independence. It should not have caught me by surprise when we entered the woods and Jason said, "It's really beautiful out here today, Dad." I stopped and looked around. Solitude. Serenity. Except for the track we left, a newly white unblemished blanket covered the forest. The brilliant blue sky contrasted that blanket to enhance its purity. The whiteness clung to the branches of every limb—indeed a winter wonderland.

This was a special place, a special time.

I looked at Jason with a sense of accomplishment and said, "It cerainly is, son." We entered the cornfield with our faces to the wind.

The day was already a success.

I peeked through the corn row for a second time. There was a nice buck in the row quartered away from us. I gently slipped into his corn row. He didn't know we were there. I inched toward him, moved into range, and he stared directly at me. I set my twenty-yard pin and released. LOW! MISSED! I paced off the distance as I approached his departure point and realized the distance was twenty-eight yards, not twenty. Bad judgment. Wait— blood! I followed the crimson trail out of the corn. The blood trail was heavy. The spots penetrated the deep snow to the ground. He was hurt! I was almost sick when I realized I had not missed, but had wounded him. Throughout my years of hunting I had harvested over thirty whitetails. I try to practice a couple of basic principles when hunting the whitetail. One is that everyone in our hunting party has an opportunity to fill his own bag. We will leave tags unfilled in this effort. The other is that you will respect the animal you are hunting. If you cannot make a clean kill, don't shoot. This shot violated that principle.

We had our work ahead of us. When we got into the pines we saw him about one hundred yards ahead of us, limping at a moderate pace. We saw him two more times as he stayed ahead of us and led us to Mom's back yard. After walking in deep snow for almost a mile, Jason was tired and we decided to stop at mom's for a bite to eat and, hopefully, to let the deer lie down. We entered Mom's back yard where Jason dropped to both knees and said, "Dad, I can't go any farther." I said "But, Jason, Grandma's house is only twenty more steps. Can I carry you?" to which he replied, "No. Just give me a minute and I can make it." Within a couple of minutes we made it to the house.

We spent the next hour eating dinner, wishing I could take back that shot, and deciding the next move. We needed to decide how far the deer intended to travel before lying down. My stepfather, Lyle, offered to drive us across the field to the other side of the woods to see if the deer had moved through. We picked up its trail on the other side. It was not going to lie down. It was headed for the swamp. The next stretch of woods was thick and hilly. I decided to trail the deer through and meet Lyle on the other side. With much reluctance, Jason went with Lyle.

As I stepped into the woods with my bow, a peculiar feeling came over me. Two hundred years ago a Native American would have felt notably confident in this situation with the equipment I had, but my confidence was not as pronounced. Instead, flashes of helplessness, mixed with tenacious determination, were flowing through my veins. I moved through the woods quietly, cautiously. The visibility was limited because of snow clinging to the trees. The feeling of solitude was overpowering. Life's complexities were forgotten. It was just the deer and I, in Mother Nature's arena of splendor.

I worked through the woods without seeing the deer. I was about to start down the cartway to meet Lyle, when I saw the buck moving in the brush ahead of me. I took off running, down the cartway, parallel to the deer and then up into the woods where I thought it would cross. I wasn't sure who would collapse first, me or the deer. Our paths finally crossed. We both slammed on the brakes and stared at each other. I drew and sank an arrow into his chest from about ten yards. He whirled around, lowered his head, and charged me. I stepped behind a tree as he fell at my feet.

The hunt was over.

Jason and Lyle came up the cartway. Jason, matter of factly, said, "Nice shot, Dad." The deer was an eight-point, two hundred-pound buck.

The day personified the beauty and the harshness of the outdoors and that fall was one that Jason and I will cherish for many years.

This was written for him to read when he gets old enough to understand that this hunt was not just about killing a deer. If I can share that experience with other dads and hunters, great.

BOB SIELING
Bertha, Minnesota

Feeding Deer Proved to Be Successful

My cousin brought me an article from a newspaper, and as I sat downstairs in my old rocking chair by the warm, cozy fireplace reading it I could not help but smile and shake my head from side to side. I let my mind drift back sixty years when I was sixteen and when I talked to the game warden about feeding deer.

As I said, when I was sixteen years old I started hunting deer east of Hinckley. Of course, I did not shoot a deer and I do not remember seeing many signs either. When the game warden checked my license very closely I asked him why so few; he replied that "the last winter had been severe and many deer had died from starvation." I asked him if it would not be possible to feed them. He said that it does not work to feed deer hay and corn—they have to eat browse. They being uniformed officers and I just a dumb farm boy, all I could do was to believe them. Several years later I brought up the subject of feeding to another game warden and his reply was about the same: if you feed deer hay and corn they would leave a trail of green slime in the snow and go off and die. Again I dropped the subject.

It was not until 1912 that we made a trip along the north shore of Minnesota to see what we could find out about how deer live in the winter. We found deer—lots of deer—that were being fed satisfactorily. The only problem was the people feeding the deer had very limited funds to purchase expensive hay and corn. I made the promise if I knew the deer would get the feed I would furnish as much as I could. This was mostly out of my own pocket. We received some donations but only a very small percent. I heard that the DNR would spend $1.1 million for the feeding program. I happen to know from experience that $1.1 million will buy a terrific amount of hay and corn.

I met a great deal of opposition from game wardens for feeding deer. I wanted to catch a deer that had only three legs and had been in almost the same spots for two days in twenty-below-zero weather and in deep snow. The game warden in that area ordered me out of the woods, saying that I was molesting the deer. I came out, but it nearly led to a vicious battle. Luckily, it didn't go that far.

I know there are a great many snowmobilers who travel on trails provided for them in northern Minnesota. I asked many of them if they wouldn't tie a bale of hay or a sack of corn to their machine and distribute it a safe distance from the trail; they more or less just laughed at me. What could be more pleasant than to travel a decent speed and see wildlife feeding along the trail?

It is correct that once you start feeding you should continue. It is also important to start feeding before the deer become too weak so they will not want to travel for food. Deer that have been fed the previous winter will usually come back to the same area, bringing their young ones with them. I knew one lady who had the same buck come back for seventeen years. She called him "Old Grey Bear." I saw for myself quite a few crippled deer that came back to the same area year after year. I especially remember one poor deer which had been shot many times, but it was in the yard eating hay and corn. I have done quite a bit of hunting, but I have not shot a great many animals. I like to be sure there are some left for next year. I do not mind shooting adult bucks, as I have seen how they chase the smaller deer away from the feed. The little ones have to run in and grab a mouthful whenever they can. I do not care to shoot a doe or a fawn and will not shoot a cow or calf moose.

I furnished feed for the deer for over twenty years and then my health gave out. I did feed deer east of Hinckley after the 1991 Halloween blizzard. That worked out very well, but I am unable to do it anymore. Feeding deer is one of the best memories I have. I say again, after so much opposition, it turns out that feeding deer is successful.

ROBERT LOFGREN
"The Old Moose Hunter"
Rush City, Minnesota

1965 Was A Year For Laughing

Our group has hunted near Big Falls for many years. We have a hunting shack located on a logging road about two miles from the highway and one mile from the end of the road. In 1965 there were five of us and we hadn't been very lucky in filling out. Only one of us, Doug, had got his deer. On the final morning we were loading up, getting ready to head home. Doug announced that he was going to the end of the road to pick up his deer where he had stashed it, and Duane decided to ride along and perhaps get one last opportunity to fill his tag.

Doug's station wagon refused to start because the battery had run down. I offered to give him a push; I had a similar station wagon of the same brand. After his was running, I suggested that if he killed the engine while loading the deer to fire a shot, and I'd come back to help him start again.

After he and Duane left, the rest of us continued loading up and were almost done when we heard a shot. He must be in trouble, I thought; we'll have to go help. I finished the loading and started for him.

Unknown to us, Duane had seen a deer, had gotten out of the truck, uncased his gun, loaded and fired, but missed. Then they continued to where Doug's deer was stashed, loaded it up, and started back where we were waiting.

As I headed for them, I saw two deer jumping across the road. By the time I got the gun uncased they were out of sight, but it alerted me to the possibility of seeing something, so I decided I'd better concentrate on looking more intently. I knew I could ignore the road in front of me; as a dead-end road it had no traffic that morning. The one vehicle down that road today was disabled with a dead battery. I proceeded slowly, giving all my attention to the woods passing by. The weather was quite mild and we'd had a little soft, slippery snow the previous night. Doug and Duane were also intently looking for deer, having completely forgotten about the shot Duane had fired and its significance to me.

As I approached a blind S curve I caught a movement out of the corner of my eye, looked up, and there was Doug's station wagon headed right for me, only a few feet away. They saw me a split second sooner, noting the expression of surprise on my face. With both vehicles' brakes locked up and sliding on the slippery new snow, there was nothing we could do to avoid the head-on collision. We hit at about five miles per hour.

So here we were out in the middle of nowhere, the only two vehicles for miles around, and we have crashed head on. Right away I was thinking of how we would feel like idiots trying to explain our stupidity. We were relieved that no one was hurt and that one vehicle would still run. I towed his wagon back to the shack where the others finally stopped laughing long enough to complete the loading. Doug said someday we too would be able to laugh about this incident, but at the time it didn't seem funny to us.

Evidently 1965 was a year for laughing because there was more to come. Doug had shot an elk in Montana and had brought the horns to the shack. He now tied those huge horns to the head of his little doe, placing the rope in such a way that it appeared to hold the deer to the fender. Only by looking very closely could you see they were not part of the deer. We drove to the restaurant in Big Falls and sat by the window to watch the reaction of the locals to that huge rack.

It was hilarious. One guy said, "That's nothing. I shot one bigger than that." The game warden drove by and did a double take, circled around, and came back.

Many walked up and wiggled the horns; some saw the ruse right away and others never did. Some recognized the truth but kept quiet in order to prolong the joke. We sat for a long time enjoying the reaction of the crowd to those phony horns. One guy said, "It must be some kind of a freak."

As I said, 1965 was a very memorable hunting season.

Max Brindos
International Falls, Minnesota

The Ace in the Hole

I began hunting deer in Marshall county in northwestern Minnesota in the late 1950s. Hunting in this area offers wide open, long-distance shooting at deer breaking between wooded areas and river bottoms. In 1985, the Conservation Reserve Program (CRP) provided another habitat for the deer by allowing land to be set aside from farming, resulting in many acres of tall grass to feed and to hide deer. To hunt in this part of the state it is best to belong to a hunting party of ten or more hunters who can drive the deer out of the woods, river bottoms, and CRP grass into open fields. My low success rate of hitting a deer running at top speed at great distances does not deter me from the thrill and fun of pursuing the whitetail.

In 1966, I began hunting with my father-in-law, Sam Radika, in St. Louis county in the northeastern part of Minnesota. Hunting these heavily wooded areas is usually done from a deer stand built in a promising spot and patiently waiting for a browsing deer to come into sight. Slashes about five feet wide lead out from the deer stand to a distance of fifty feet or so, to provide the hunter with a shooting lane. I favor this type of hunting because it frequently offers an easy shot at a walking or standing animal. I hunted with Sam until 1980 before I returned to the northwestern part of the state.

I never owned a rifle during my first few years of hunting and would borrow one from friends during the season. When I finally decided to buy my first deer rifle, my wife and I agreed on a new 30-30 Winchester Centennial, which we looked at and which I admired. When the salesman went to get a new one from storage, a kindly man who had been observing and perhaps listening to us, asked if I intended to shoot the rifle or to look at it. I understood his meaning—did I want a rifle for the woods or a showpiece? We left the store before the salesman returned and I remembered that lesson ever since, because when I bought rifles for myself, my daughter, and my son, they were all used rifles. I bought a used 30-30 Winchester in 1967 for $65, and it was more than adequate when hunting with Sam, until I sold it in 1972 for $50. I then bought a used 30-06 Remington Model

740 for $100, and my first shots from this rifle were very memorable.

The 1972 season was a short one for me because my workload reduced it to one weekend. I didn't have time to sight in my "new" rifle before driving up north to Sam's place and when we didn't see any deer on Saturday, I thought it may not matter. On Sunday as the sun started to set in the west and the shadows began to play tricks on my eyes, I thought that soon the season would be over and I'd have to wait a full year to use my 30-06. Sam had come out with me that afternoon but did not take a stand; he preferred to mooch around. That was fortunate for me becaues he crossed a road and went into another wooded area north of me to scare up deer for me.

The first deer to cross the road and to follow the trail leading to my stand was a doe that ran straight for me only to veer away at the last second, bringing it broadside and only ten yards from me. When I shot, I hit it high on the back, which dropped the doe instantly. The second deer was an eight-point buck following closely behind. For a second I did not know what to do; this rifle had no lever to work and I was accustomed to a lever. This deer stood there, looking directly at me. I snapped out of mental lapse quicker than the buck snapped out of his surprise and I thought, where would I aim, because I had never sighted in this rifle. I aimed between his eyes and that's excactly where the bullet hit; it dropped to its knees, exactly the way I had seen my grandfather shoot steers for butchering.

I turned back to the doe and put a mercy shot in it and called to Sam to come help me dress out these two deer. When he came across the road, I knew he had indeed been the one to scare them into my range. As he approached me and saw the two deer within a ten-yard triangle of my stand, he asked, "But where's the third deer?" I said, "What are you talking about?" To that he replied, "I heard three shots." To that I retorted "Only two deer came out and there they are."

I enjoyed the many years I hunted with Sam and, although I thought he might be getting too old to continue hunting, I had another reason to return to the northwestern part of the state to hunt in 1980. I wanted to establish myself with my younger brother and his hunting party. My concern that Sam was too old to hunt was baseless because when my daughter and son were old enough to hunt, Sam was still hunting and began hunting with them, too. My other reason was timely because hunting land was getting scarce, and my brother, Bruce, was hunting with some area farmers who had access to hunting land. Over the years our group gained and lost hunting buddies of the original crew, besides Bruce and me, there is Leonard Stoltman and his five sons, Michael, Gayle, Glenn, Mark, and Preston plus Ralph Przybylski, Milt Smidt, and Phil Sprague. An incident that happened to me in 1982 was remembered over the years and played a key role in establishing a name for our hunting group, including holding an annual election for president. The honor of being president still is a dubious one when you learn how the club got its name.

In 1982, our first drive was an opening day in a wooded area about eighty acres in size. We called it "The Ace In the Hole" because we could always count on driving deer from this small area. We had about thirteen hunters in our party that morning and each was given an assignment: drivers, front and back posters, and flankers.

I was given a choice assignment, being a front poster on the northwest corner of the woods. This spot was good because farther north and west was a larger wooded area out of which deer liked to break. Drivers also liked this area because it was sparse enough to get some shooting inside those woods. This morning was no exception when the drivers began driving the woods behind me from the south; some early shooting was heard.

The first hunt of the year was underway.

When the drivers were halfway through the woods, three deer appeared near the end of the wood where I was posted. I could see them clearly in a ten-foot cut made years ago for a fence line. The deer always hesitated at that point, apparently to assess their options. They saw the other poster at the east end and me at the west end and pranced nervously for a long time before breaking out in my direction. The first deer was a good-sized buck with two does. They headed yards away when I took aim at the buck. When my first shot missed I was still patient and careful but missed again. By this time the buck and does were one hundred yards away and moving rapidly in powerful bounding strides. My third and fourth shots didn't score either, and I was wondering what I was doing wrong. I put my spare clip in the rifle, reloaded the empty clip, and composed myself, remaining ready because the drivers were still working the woods. As they were finishing their drive, three more deer appeared at the same place and I thought God was being good to me, allowing me a chance for atonement. However, God turned out to be more of a humorist than I expected and the prior situation repeated itself. I've always believed hunting is a sport where the hunter can be made fun of, so I was ready to tell my partners the whole truth and take my ribbing, harassment, badgering, and bandering, no matter how painful it might become.

This fiasco became the cornerstone to naming our deer hunting club. When Glenn Stoltman gave out the asssignments for our next day's hunt, he waited until all the party members had an assignment before he looked at me. Then loudly, so everyone would be sure to hear, he said, "Gale, you go over by Radium and post." Radium is as tiny village about five miles away. He was practically banning me!

In 1974, to add to the spirit and camaraderie of our club, Bruce Anderson bought a plaque for our club and had a logo with our name, "Radium Club," placed on it, plus twelve brass nameplates upon which we would engrave the presidents' names and years of service.

My skills over the past two years didn't improve too much, and I was elected the club's first president.

Not to take my honor lightly, I prepared a manual for each member, which included a charter, a list of charter members, a mission statement, a deer hunters' code, and something we called Buck Points. These points were given out for any screwups, regardless of the cause—mental, physical, technical, or mechanical. Some examples are shooting a small deer, sleeping/dozing, missing an open standing sjot, not sighting in a rifle, having a dirty capped scope when ready to shot. A lot of politicking goes on during a hunt, particularly by those piling up points against themselves, attempting to exaggerate the Buck Points other members should be assessed. The retiring president was responsible for having the incoming president's name and tenure entered on the plaque and delivered to his home, where it was required to be prominently displayed until the next season, much to the new man's chagrin. As first president, did I ever redeem myself for that ordeal at The Ace In the Hole? Let's fast forward to 1989 to see how the story ends.

Once again our hunting party gathered at The Ace In the Hole. All the assignments were made and I was given the same posting spot only this time I was relegated to being a back poster. A safe place for me, I thought; while the drivers were lining up at the north end of the drive I was making my way to the northwest corner to take my place as a back poster.

I stood there waiting for about five minutes, while the drivers were starting to make their drive to the south. While waiting there I noticed a sturdy-looking fence post, which would make a good steadying post, if necessary for the rifle. I strolled over to it, which brought me close to a red willow thicket where I heard a thrashing sound I knew could only be a deer breaking out. My few extra steps apparently had spooked a nearby deer, which apparently had been watching me, wondering what I was up to.

I thought the deer would head to the west, keeping the red willows between us, but no, it ran east, keeping itself parallel to me and only twenty yards away. I could see that it was a big buck carrying a huge rack. Only a crafty old buck would hold out in a small thicket. I quickly got him in my sights and proceeded to miss him on my first two shots. Deja vu! If I came up empty-handed again, I could never face my buddies for missing this monster. On my third shot, I dropped it and felt an enormous relief.

Locating the downed buck in the CRP grass caused me some anxious minutes because I remembered stories of bucks crawling on their knees to escape to safety. Finally with help from the other back poster, Michael, we located the buck and saw that beautiful thirteen-point rack.

The drivers had just entered the woods when I had started shooting and they didn't know what had happened.

Michael drove over to them with their gun cases and told them of my big buck. I had help field-dressing the buck, and two of us took it to the waiting gang. When I appeared in the back of the pickup with my buck, they all stood in formation with their hands out, taking deep bows, and saying "Big kahuna." My humiliation of the past years was healing and, while I know it will never be totally erased, bagging a buck with a thirteen-point rack was a good start. They encouraged me to have it mounted by Milt Smidt, who does taxidermy, and I agreed because the next January I would turn fifty years old and who knows if I will ever get a shot at such a buck again.

Did I ever get elected president again? Yes, but that's another story.

GALE J. ANDERSON
Bloomington, Minnesota

Roughing It at Lake Fourteen

Just as the East has its Adirondacks, Minnesota has its Range.

Many years ago a well-to-do Chicago family, burned by the sweltering summer heat, decided to build a summer cottage in northern Minnesota, to which they must have been familiar. Maybe a year-round place they said.

They intentionally looked for a site in the heart of the Range, in the Up North country, called the Range because it was part of the great Mesabi Iron Ore Range, which was strung out underground among many cities. Hence, the people came to be known as Rangers.

About twenty miles north of Virginia they found a beautiful crescent-shaped lake sometimes called "Crescent" and sometimes "Lake Fourteen"; here they bought some lakeshore land and built what they thought would be a year-round cottage, complete with three bedrooms. Although they ignored the need for insulation, they tried to fight the coming cold with wooden exterior and tongue-and-groove interior walls, hoping those would do the trick. Stupido!

When they went back to Chicago with tails between their legs, probably frozen during the first August, Henry and Emma Hanson of Virginia bought the place. They spent countless summers there and gradually improved the property.

Each spring Henry moved Emma and the girls, Lucille and Carol, to The Lake for the summer, while he commuted daily from his Virginia business, the Range Paper company, where he prospered.

Carol, now my spouse of fifty-two years, remembers the annual trek, how they loaded the Buick with summertime items, such as sheets, lightweight blankets, towels, clothing, *ad infinitum*. Also, Aunt Louise.

Emma's maiden sister, Aunt Louise, had joined the family from the very beginning. In fact, local rumor said she had probably accompanied the couple on their honeymoon. But, not to put down Louise, in years she became the family seamstress, particularly for Lucille's family, the first girl married and the first to have children with their constant need of clothing. Louise was a godsend. As the sisters, Lucille and Carol, grew into their teens, they enjoyed many parties at The Lake, where they were practically prisoners with high school friends from Virginia coming out regularly for parties. Twenty miles from town was a sizeable distance then.

Through the years, Lucille, mother of the new generation, became the spaghetti master of the Range. At the drop of a hat, as an adult, she could produce a huge meal of homemade spaghetti sauce, and many an impromptu dance or card party was consummated with spaghetti gorging. .

This ability was to be admired in a non-Italian living amongst a large Italian population.

Those were the years when some major renovations occurred. The very enjoyable screened-in porch around two sides of the house was eliminated on one side to provide a full dining room and an extension of the living room with its large fireplace. But the full porch on the lake side remained, with its superb view of the water and its ample supply of wicker furniture, which endured through the years.

A garage near the road remained, as did a woodshed for tools, an icehouse, and a boathouse down by the lake.

Running water was available by kitchen pump, with the water level being barely below the ground surface level. But the Chic Sale remained along a path into the woods. The telephone and electricity was still a way off.

This is the situation, the setting, when I first saw The Lake.

Carol and I were married in 1943 and, by invitation, spent our honeymoon there, compliments of Henry and Emma.

I had experienced a lot of camp supervisory experience, was an Eagle Scout, and greatly enjoyed our first family days at The Lake.

However, I faced surprises.

I had never heard of a family icehouse. To me an icehouse was a community commercial place where three hundred-pound slabs of ice were loaded on a distributor's truck, driven by a man wearing a heavy leather jacket and owning a big pair of tongs. This was different. This icehouse was a shed about the size of grandpa's smokehouse and was full of ice. Contractors came around in the winter, cut huge blocks of ice from Lake Fourteen in front of the house, dragged them to the ice house and packed them heavily in sawdust, where the ice tried to last through the summer. Even in August 1943 that icehouse still held a fourth of its winter harvest. It was my job to dig around in that damp sawdust, to find a piece of ice, and carry it to the icebox like the men in town did, using identical tongs. The reader must realize that all the time I was in that damp icehouse, I was remembering the snakes in Uncle Seborn's barn on the banks of the Lamine River in Missouri. But there didn't seem to be any snakes in Minnesota. Thank God.

Of course, the place went through many changes, and generations. When the Hansons died, the two daughters, Lucille and Carol, jointly inherited it. My Carol sold (practically gave) her half to Aunt Louise who was still alive and lived at The Lake each summer. Years later, Louise now dead, Lucille and Einer inherited the place as sole owners, and it was their turn to update portions of the place.

Electricity and telephone had now come down the road, which truly made modernization possible. Telephone, television, electric cooking, refrigeration, lights, were now easily possible. Even a modern bathroom created at the end of the long front porch facing the lake, was engineered. But no one wanted to destroy the old Chic Sale. It had been a friend, a refuge, for too many years.

Soon the old boathouse was moved to the opposite end of the lakeshore and converted into a sauna, that Finnish steam bath greatly appreciated by Rangers of all nationalities. To sit in a sauna (men-only or women-only, at times) and to sweat to your desired level of pink, followed by a cooling down by pouring lake-temperature water over your naked body, or if you must be a traditionalist, by running out on the dock to jump into the lake buck naked, which was invigorating as all hell, but it was not for the poor of heart. And a nearby bed was highly recommended.

Sometimes after a sauna, Einer (Lucille's husband) would honor the new tradition of having a bedtime brandy, which only enhanced the deep sleep to come. The brandy had replaced Henry's Haig & Haig scotch many years previously.

So that's where we spent our honeymoon, and future summers for many years after 1943, when our lovely daughters, Judith and Pauline, enjoyed our annual trip to The Lake for a few weeks. Being a schoolteacher during those years, time was available to me during the summers.

Yes, our family has only *great* and *good* memories of The Lake. Infant Judith sitting in the path to the house (photo by Dad), Judith and cousin Gayle (Lucille and Einer's daughter) swimming and playing in the surf at nearby Lake Leander, Judith being pushed off the dock by stupid Dad to encourage learning to swim, daughter Pauline learning to paint there and also all of us fishing; in later years, Dad leading a parade of lakers on his big Suzuki 750 on the annual Fourth of July parade around the lake.

Even though The Lake place was in a fairly populous area, with lots of undeveloped area nearby, I can't remember much successful deer hunting using The Lake as a hunting headquarters. To be sure, I walked the roads and the trails a few times, without success, but it was largely a matter of walking leisurely through woods I knew intimately. Perhaps Einer and son Bruce headquartered there once or twice before I came into the family, but I think not. I discussed this with Gayle Anderson Miller, Einer's second daughter, and neither of us can dredge up a memory of a deer being strung up after the kill at The Lake.

And we can't forget the berries. Blueberries growing wild all over the property; wild raspberries gathering dust along the gravel roadside, a Juneberry tree just where you turned off the road into the property, and fish.

All over this world, people know of Minnesota's walleye, the great native fish; people from miles away were enticed to come to Minnesota to fish. How well I remember trolling around the lake at the end of the day with father-in-law Henry, working on crappies. Henry, with his white office shirt. It was said that even when he had gone to Canada years ago or to the Ely area, with first son-in-law Einer, that he always wore white shirts, because, as a businessman, that's what he traditionally wore, and he was happy with them.

Nothing is more typical of Minnesota than the fish, unless it's the deer! Even Judith forgave Dad, years later, for pushing her off the dock, when she remembered how excellently old Dad could prepare fish by pan-frying or by roasting over an outdoor fire at The Lake. Or even at home.

Today The Lake seems empty and deserted. We get there only about every third summer. Lucille and Einer's little children's voices are no longer heard there. Neither are our daughters' voices; they're all adults. Some of their children's voices might yell and screech there (great grandchildren of the Hansons)—but they're grown, too. Awaiting another generation, the place is now owned by Bruce, son of Lucille and Einer, grandson of Henry and Emma.

It's more than just the lake cottage. It's The Lake. It's the place my Carol spent her summers as a teenager, to which she returned as a young bride and, eventually, as a young mother. A place of much love and memories.

A place forever.

A place Up North.

WILLIAM H. HULL
Edina, Minnesota

Hunting Until Nearly Dark Pays Off

The woods were coming to life as the early morning light filtered through the trees to the east. The soothing call of the mild-mannered chickadees was soon drowned out by the continuous bantering of a pair of blue jays, whose blaring calls were intense and overbearing. Even though I enjoyed their beautiful coloration, I was grateful to see them leave. The brisk November breeze felt good on my exposed face. It was like Mother Nature's morning cup of coffee. I was already on a natural high, though, from the exhiliration of being back out in the woods taking part in the long-awaited annual deer season. I was hunting in classic midwestern farm country, land dominated by large corn and soybean fields intermixed with small ten- to forty-acre woodlots and sloughs. With the numerous farms in this area, it was zoned for shotgun hunting only.

With the majority of the corn still standing, I predicted that this was going to be a tough season. The deer learn quickly that the dense stands of corn provide better cover than the open woodlots. With the demands of running my own business, I couldn't afford the time to do much preseason scouting so, for opening morning, I decided to return to where I had harvested a fine doe the previous season. This was a twenty-acre selection of hardwoods surrounded by a large swamp on one side and fields on the other side.

As the morning continued, so did the muffled shots in the distance. With the breeze it was hard to tell from which direction those shots were coming, but I hoped at least one came from the slough, about a mile away, where my uncle was hunting.

By late morning the Minnesota chill had already numbed my feet. With the lack of any deer sightings, and the nagging ache of ten frozen toes, I decided to climb down from my tree limb and try some still hunting. As I walked I hoped to find some reassuring deer sign. The slow, methodical pace revealed a new scene with every step. The three inches of fresh snow was ideal for this style of hunting. It was just enough to quiet the underlayer of crisp leaves. Out of the corner of my eye I caught a quick blur of motion, which turned out to be a red fox that came bouncing along less than fifteen yards in front of me. I had eluded the keen senses of this fellow hunter. As I watched its thick billowy tail disappear into the brush, I thought to myself that the day was already a success.

With the rut in full swing it didn't take too long to find a handful of fresh scrapes and rubs. Most of them were typical in size but I found three scrapes, which truly excited me. I know that you can't accurately determine the size of a buck by the size of the scrape, but the general rule of thumb is that the bigger the scrape, the bigger the buck. All three of these scrapes were about seven feet long by five feet wide. This is strong indication that I was standing in the middle of a large buck's territory. I knew these scrapes weren't made by any forkhorn. In addition to these, I found a rub on a maple tree which was about eight inches in diameter. Indeed there was a very big buck around here someplace. Incidentally, I noticed that only one of the scrapes had been freshened up since the previous night's snowfall. So I decided to get my portable tree stand and set up adjacent to the two unvisited scrapes for the evening hunt.

Upon returning to the area in the early afternoon, I located a nice straight-trunk oak on which I attached my stand. It was within forty yards of each scrape. As I settled in for the evening, the breeze all but disappeared. The sights and sounds were so relaxing that I almost forgot why I was out there. Turning my head as slowly as my patience would allow, I scanned my shooting zone. Since there was no real trail leading to the scrapes, and the breeze had died down, I had no idea from which direction a deer would come, if one came at all.

As I watched the placid surroundings, I was amused by the antics of a nearby partridge that was foraging for berries. It would hop from branch to branch, consuming all the berries within reach; the further it ventured, the lower the branch would sag. It browsed most of the evening. Then, just before dusk, it thundered away to some unknown roosting site.

Once again, I couldn't understand the lack of deer movement in the area. By this time I should have seen at least a doe or two visiting the scrapes to leave their calling cards. I decided I'd sit only another five minutes, turning my head around trying to pick out any detail in the fading light. I was searching for the horizontal back line or even a twitching ear. Nothing.

Then my eyes came to rest on the full body of a large buck. It startled me because I had heard nothing. Yet, here he was, broadside to me and nose to the ground. It was as if he had appeared out of thin air. He was about sixty yards from me and slowly walking toward the scrapes. He turned his head and looked directly away from me. I had a good look at his massive rack and couldn't believe how wide it was. As he resumed his silent approach, I eased the 870 to my shoulder. I hadn't realized how badly I was shaking unil I looked down the barrel. It was swaying back and forth, left to right, like a flag in the wind. I told myself to breathe deeply, which only caused my chest to start gurgling. The closer the buck came, the louder my chest became. I knew I had to end this soon or I was going to keel over from the anxiety.

The buck had sulked behind a group of three trees, so I decided to take him when he reappeared on the other side. But he never came out.

I waited for what seemed an eternity. Had he vanished as suddenly as he had appeared? Suddenly a cloud of dirt appeared from behind the trees. Instead of visiting the existing scrapes, he was making a fourth one. I decided to lean out from my stand as far as I could, so I would be able to see around the trees. As I did this, the stand let out a disclosing creak. The buck instantly turned toward me and stared.

It was at me, as if we were exchanging an immense respect between our roles as predator and prey.

He crumpled with the echo of my shot. For a moment we became as one in the beautiful life and death cycle of nature.

As the last rays of twilight faded, I walked silently to my trophy, knelt down beside that magnificent animal, and rested my hand on his still body. I felt the familiar mixed emotions that only a hunter understands.

It was over.

SCOTT S. FROEMMING
Crystal, Minnesota

The Buck That Got Away

About fifteen years ago my son, Gary, told me I should get a bigger deer rifle after many years hunting with a 30-30 Winchester Model 64 that had never failed me. He said I needed a bigger gun if I ever decided to go elk hunting. After much thought, I decided to get a Browning lever-action .308. With it I purchased a 1.5x5 Leopold duplex scope and targeted the gun at one hundred yards. It shot an excellent group and seemed to be the ideal gun for deer hunting.

There was one little problem with the hammer that didn't seem to be very important. When I released the hammer with my thumb, it would sometimes catch a little. It didn't seem to be very serious so I didn't pay much attention to it. That was a serious mistake.

Two weeks before the season opening, my son and I went to Nevis, Minnesota, to build our deer stands. I built mine in a pine tree overlooking a buck scrape about twenty-five yards away in a deer trail which ran alongside an old, abandoned fence line.

I was in my stand before daylight on opening morning. It was fairly cold at twenty degrees, but I figured I could stand the cold for most of the day. Nothing happened until about noon when I heard the telltale noise of a deer headed my way. I couldn't believe my eyes when the buck of a lifetime stepped into that scrape twenty-five yards away. Not a limb or a branch stood between me and that ten-pointer with a perfect rack, a ten-point buck with a perfect set of horns which undoubtedly would have field dressed at about 225 pounds. All I had to do was to put the crosshairs, pull the trigger, and that buck was mine. I knew he didn't have a chance of one in a thousand of getting away. He was mine! I could see his head mounted and hanging on my wall.

As he stopped, I cocked the gun, raised it to my shoulder, and centered the crosshairs on his ribs, just back of his shoulder, and pulled the trigger.

Nothing happened.

About this time I would have given anything for my trusty Model 64.

I took the gun down from my shoulder and looked at the action. Nothing wrong. It was cocked and ready to go. Once more I drew down on the buck and pulled he trigger. Again, nothing. By this time I was getting desperate and the buck knew something was going on. Time was running out.

The third time I raised the rifle, the buck got his eyes on me and with a frantic jerk on the trigger and the same nonresult, he let out a very loud snort and left a very sick and disgusted hunter behind.

I should have wrapped the gun around a tree or given it to the first hunter who walked by, but I didn't. But I did take it to a local gunsmith after we returned home.

No, it wasn't buck fever. It was the gun. After thoroughly checking it out, he decided that the button that releases the hammer didn't release because the lever didn't push the button up far enough. It worked fine when the weather was warm, but when it was cold, it simply wouldn't fire. A major defect. He filed a little off the lever so it would push the button up a little more and release the hammer when the trigger was pulled.

Now I'm well satisfied with the gun, having bagged seven deer with it after that day fifteen years ago.

But I'll never forget that once-in-a-lifetime buck that got away.

RODNEY WESTERGREN
Bertha, Minnesota

Young Hunters Weren't Prepared

When I was a teenager going to high school in El Paso, Texas, I had two very good friends, Gene and David, both now deceased. The three of us did just about everything together, quail hunting, fishing in the Rio Grande, and just camping out.

One year we decided that deer hunting should be our next experience. None of us owned rifles so it was first necessary to learn from whom we could borrow them.

We then loaded all gear in a 1926 Model T Ford, which we jointly owned, and headed for Sierra Blanca, Texas, which is about ninety miles southeast of El Paso, Texas, where we had been told there were deer.

When we arrived in the area we simply parked our car along the highway and took off toward the nearest range of hills. This area is generally desert and cactus country with some scrub trees. We walked, feeling like mighty hunters, but without seeing a deer for two or three miles into the desert.

Suddenly on a ridge just ahead of us we spotted a lovely young buck. Now what do we do? Only my friend, David, seemed without awe as he simply dropped to the ground, brought up his rifle and CRACK, dropped that animal with the one shot.

Needless to say we were all dumfounded, including David. We ran to see our prey and, sure enough, that one shot had killed him.

The question now became, what do we do with him? I don't think it had even seriously entered our minds that we might end up with a real deer.

We knew that it should be dressed out, but none of us had the slightest idea of how to accomplish that task, even if one of us had a knife to try.

Then the next question was how to get our trophy back to the car. We thought of tying him to some kind of pole and carrying him on our shoulders, but, alas, the west Texas desert has very few trees, even had we had an axe, which we didn't.

We could think of only one solution and that was literally to drag that deer across the sand by afffixing our belts to his horns, and with the three of us pulling mightily, we dragged that deer two and a half miles across the desert to our car.

The next question was whether we could get it back to El Paso in time for some experienced person to dress it out. It was a typical Texas warm day, but we got our Model T going as fast as it could and headed for home.

Much to our relief we did get back in time for David's brother to dress out the deer and save the meat. Obviously the hide was useless after two and one-half miles of sandy abrasion.

Our escapade was even noted by the local newspaper, and I still have a copy of the photo with the three hunters standing proudly by our Model T.

Although I left El Paso shortly after finishing high school and David moved to Alaska, our first deer hunt was something none of us ever forgot and laugh about whenever we had the chance to meet in later years.

The nature of our friendship was evident in that it was always referred to as "our" deer and "our deer hunt," even though, strictly speaking, it was David's deer.

JOHN G. KRESSEL
Edina, Minnesota

Whose Buck Was It Anyway?

I am a very avid bow and gun deer hunter. For the last eleven years, I have used the bow almost exclusively and have bagged nine deer. I have encouraged two of my friends, Russell and Robby, to try bow hunting and see how peaceful and beautiful it can be sitting up in a tree and see nature and wildlife at its best.

Our big day started with me picking up the other two and driving to the woods we were to hunt. As we were readying our bows, I was putting scent on each of us and telling the two beginners the directions to get to their stands, emphasizing that the direction of the wind was a very big factor in getting to see the deer. We were in our stands hours before the prime time to get settled down.

As I had gone to my stand the two previous times, I had met up with an eight-point buck both times and just hoped I'd see him again and hopefully this time get off a shot. First, a doe came by and I let her go, and I noticed she continued in the direction where Robby would be. Not long after that the eight-pointer came by again and the standoff began. He came within seven yards of me, stopped, and looked straight at me. I couldn't move—I didn't dare to do so; I thought, This is the third time this has happened and I don't want to strike out. Just as I shot, the buck turned around and I could see the arrow penetrate his left hind quarter.

I followed the blood trail in the direction of Robby and I started to think that maybe Robby or Russell got a shot at the doe or maybe even at the buck I had shot. I got there and the two guys were on the ground trying to find Robby's arrows he had shot at the doe.

He said, "I don't know how I could have missed. I could have jumped on it and every time I shot at it, it didn't move. I shot three times and missed and then this buck came by and looked like he was hurting."

I then told them, "That's the buck I hit!" and I could see the gleam in their eyes to go after it and trail it. Also I could see Robby's disgust that he had missed the doe. Knowing the buck was already dead (because I had seen it die) I sent Robby and

Russell in the direction of the buck and said maybe they could get a shot at it because by this time it could be weak or even bedded down — and they could get the killing shot.

I stood behind a tree and watched as the two began to follow the blood trail. It was fun watching them find and then lose the trail of the wounded deer. They yelled to me "EEK-EEK" [my nickname] "it's here and it's a nice eight-pointer. We've found it."

To this day they claim I never would have found it and that I was going in the wrong direction when trailing it. But only if they knew.

When we get together now, it's always fun reliving this hunt, but I still don't have the heart to tell them I knew where it was lying and that it was already dead.

LARRY UIECKER
Gaylord, Minnesota

A 1937 Hunt at Lake Christine

My dad, Chester Le Roy "Mac" McNelly, first discovered the Arrowhead district as a college student and part-time summer worker when he was asked to do some timber survey work about 1907. He wrote of it in one of the booklets he published. I think his first excursion into Lake Christine was in 1927 or 1928, when he was invited to join a hunting group led by a Mr. Clinch, who owned a small cabin on the west shore of Lake Christine.

To get to the lake was an experience, in those early days of 1907. The only route would have been to walk from the North Shore Trail (even though it was only an Indian trail at that time) and through the pristine forest. Access during his first hunting trips in the 1920s was by Model T Ford, about fourteen miles up Honeymoon Trail, which headed directly north from Lutsen, and connected with the Sawbill road. Between them, one did a lot of zigzagging including a couple of switchbacks where, according to his tales of the early jaunts, one really had to "thread the needle" and pay strict attention or one wound up in the quagmire with little chance of getting help to push or lift the car out of the mud or snow. His histories of those early trips were exciting, as he told of meeting the other members of his hunting group at Lutsen and taking that precarious trip "in train" (as he called it) to cope with the hazards. The road at that time was a rough track up and down hillsides, barely wide enough and often with underbrush closing in on both sides of the car. There was no curb, no gutter, no paving, no grading. You actually drove through the wild and rough forest dodging rocks and stumps, if you could, or straddling them if you thought they were low enough. If a tree had fallen over the track, you got out and muscled it out of the way, or found a way around it. The road was on a slant with one side of the car precariously higher than the other side. The danger was that when it was wet or icy, you could slide off the road before you knew it or could prevent it. There were many ways you could wind up in deep trouble, especially in the winter time in that remote country.

Mr. Clinche had a position at the University of Minnesota Agricultural college, where Pop had his office, and Mr. Clinche had invited Pop and others to hunt from the cabin where he had homesteaded years earlier. I never met the gentleman, because by the time I reached hunting age he had passed on, but his first trip there was in 1937, the year I was fifteen. I wouldn't be old enough to get a hunting license until the next year, but Pop thought I needed the experience before he would allow me to carry a gun. Incidentally, a license and a deer tag in the thirties cost $1, permitting the licensee to shoot either a doe or a buck, plus a bear and, I think, a moose, which we rarely saw anyhow.

By this time the best route to the cabin was to go up the North Shore drive, one mile past Lutsen, turn north at the schoolhouse toward Elk lake, (or was it Moose lake?) resort. This route was a comparative breeze, the first four miles basically due north, up a graded gravel road, then where the resort road created a "Y" to the right, take the left fork over a more primitive dirt road, which soon became more like the Honeymoon trail, a mere ungraded track with a log of sidehill driving and rock dodging for much of the last four miles, crossing over three small wooden bridges before coming to the first glimpse of the south shore of Lake Christine. From there it was a mere quarter of a mile around the west side and up the hill. The cabin was down by the shore, on our right; we drove off the road in case of a snowstorm, and walked our duffle down the last couple of hundred feet down to the cabin.

Mr. Clinche's cabin was a rather small affair, considering there were usually six or eight of us. There was a main room, about twelve by sixteen feet, where we cooked, ate, and socialized, a small backroom where a few slept, and a loft up a rickety stair, where the rest of us slept. There was a window upstairs, a small one that let in a little light during the daytime, but the whole place was always a little spooky. The cabin was sheathed for some reason in steel sheeting which, by this time, was thoroughly rusted, with the appearance of utter disrepute. Really "rustic." We used it only a very short time until it collapsed in about 1948.

But before that 1948 collapse, I had been in the party and started going along with my dad in 1937, thereafter having all the benefits and obligations of being one of the crew. Let me tell you more details about the camp.

Our water source was Lake Christine; we supplied ourselves by dipping a bucket into the lake. Years previously someone had rolled a couple of very large rocks just far enough into the water that their tops were exposed as stepping stones, and it was possible to scoop the bucket from that point. That water was the sweetest ever and cold. We didn't give a thought to contamination then, since it was part of God's own creation, still completely pure. The only people who lived on the lake at that time were a Mr. and Mrs. Stone, a middle-aged couple who lived on the far north side and us for a week or so once a year.

There was no outhouse. We just took a small supply of toilet paper out in the woods with us. At that we were berated for being soft and citified, the old soldiers insisting they used catalog pages. I didn't see proof of anything in that attitude.

On the first evening at sundown it was traditional to take a .22 rifle and shoot a partridge or two from one of the low branches of nearby evergreens, to flavor the hunters' stew until real meat came our way, usually by the next evening. This partridge hunt required about ten or fifteen minutes even by the rawest recruit, since partridge and grouse were plentiful and not spooked easily at that time of day. The stew contained, beside the birds, a lot of potatoes, carrots, onions, maybe a a few beggies, some cabbage, and whatever else we had brought along to cook. It was sacrilege to bring any meat, other than bacon, which was only for breakfast with eggs. The superstition was that we were here to hunt and that we might hex our luck with any store-bought meat. We always had deer meat to plop into the stew by noon of the second day, if not the first morning, a part of the first kill being traditionally sacrificed for that purpose.

My dad always bought the staples we needed and did the cooking. He liked doing it but always warned us that if anyone complained he would automatically become the cook. We were careful to praise the stew, the breakfast pancakes, burned or not, and any other food offered. Each of us chipped in our share of the total costs, which usually worked out to be about 67 cents per man per trip. We didn't assign duties except for washing or drying dishes. Chopping firewood, carrying water and such duties were done easily by volunteers usually working in pairs. Pop usually arrived first in camp so he could control his schedule. He would already have destroyed rat and mice nests, swept out any porcupine needles, started the fire, drawn the first bucket of water, maybe even patched a leaky roof, and be there to greet us, like a family member.

There were some very fine men who hunted with us, or I should say I hunted with them. Among them were Carl Ashe, a county agent, a great guy who always brought along a fifteen-gallon milk can full of excellent buttermilk, which we all enjoyed, plus he brought a bale of straw for mattresses. There was a Mr. Ghant who went out of his way to take me to camp one season and was also a tobacco chewer. A Mr. Palmer, another county agent whom I thought remarkable because he first saw any work to be done and quietly did it. Also a Schule Rutford, whose parents had emigrated from Iceland; hence, I could understand his strange name. Then there was a Mr. Hoxi, in his eighties, Schule's father-in-law. We stored the shack's windows and barrel stove in his garage in Duluth; they wouldn't have been safe in that remote area.

These men, along with my brother Dean and a couple of select high school buddies were the chief actors in my hunting experiences. My older brothers had hunted in earlier years but had left our part of the world by this time.

R. K. McNelly Sr.
Edina, Minnesota

Three Bucks for Me in 1951

The first year I started deer hunting was 1951, north of Pillager, Minnesota. I've had lots of exciting experiences doing it ever since. We had a deer camp south of Remer in the fifties and sixties until we moved the camp, a railroad boxcar, north of Effie in Craigsville in 1971. My fondest memories of hunting deer occurred there. My father and his two friends from Brainerd, Roy Larson and Ping Peerington, arrived on Thursday and set up the camp so all was prepared.

When I was driving up north on Thursday all I could hear on the radio was storm warnings. A severe winter storm was moving into North Dakota and then on into northern Minnesota. That kind of weather makes hunters nervous up north, particularly those who were caught in the great Armistice day storm of November 11, 1940.*

I had rebuilt my deer stand in mid-October with the help of my fourteen-year-old daughter. It was at the edge of a four hundred-acre clear cut area. I had earlier discovered that a storm had felled the tree in which my stand was built, so I had to build a new one. It was some distance from our camp. I had to walk approximately a mile from camp, through the woods, and across a large beaver dam flooded area, then up through another old Christmas tree trail, deep in the woods to my stand. I had even trimmed leaves and twigs along the path to hold down the noise; I could almost walk to the stand unseen and without a sound.

It was comfortable in the lodge when I arrived there Thursday night. The wood-burning stove was putting out some heat and the gaslights gave off a warm yellow glow. The talk, of course, was about the coming storm and how it might affect us. Finally to sleep.

Friday started to be nice except for the driving rain when we got up at 3:30 A.M., built up the fire, had a bite of breakfast, and got dressed for the miserable day. The woods were very quiet because of the wet ground. We prepared for the day by packing wood into the shack for a quick fire when we returned, by packing ourselves a light lunch, and determining where each hunter was to go for the day. There were about eleven of us, mainly people who had hunted together for twenty-five years or so, my brothers, brother-in-law, my dad, and other friends, the LaVasseurs from Farmington and Virginia, Minnesota. Late in the afternoon it became very blustery. By the time we were ready to go we had a driving rain. Phooey.

Just before we left I went to the car to get my Winchester Model 100; I quickly put the lens cover on the scope so it wouldn't fog up in all that humidity. Then I donned my bright yellow rain pants and an orange camouflage raincoat and left for my stand.

There were so many trees blown down on my trail that it took forty-five minutes to reach my stand. I frequently realized I had lost the guide marks I had blazed on a few trees and had to back-track to find the trail. The tree stand was solid ice. I had to mount it by a short ladder and a couple of spikes driven into the tree for footholes. I cleared off the seat of this big old spruce. Then I waited. It was so overcast it wasn't until about 7:10 A.M. before it was light enough to shoot, and a heavy snowfall had started mixing in with the rain. Trees were being blown down all around me; I could see only about 250 yards, at which point the snowflakes blended everything into a fog.

Then off to my left I noticed something.

Out from the trees coming through the clear-cut area, I could pick out a buck, not huge, but respectable, with about three points. Nice forked horns. As he was about 140 yards away, I took a shot and got him. He was down and out. My scope didn't fog up either, much to my surprise, so I quickly covered the scope lens again. I waited for a while before I went down to gut the buck. I had just rolled it over for better drainage before re-turning to my stand in the tree. I didn't want to repeat last year's experience. I had just shot a buck when shortly two or three other deer came following him, and I couldn't move fast enough to get another shot.

I sat there for several minutes or so, and it was a little after eight o'clock. I wondered whether I should go down, drag my deer to another trail, or would I have to drag it about a mile? I could reach it with an all-terrain vehicle.

As I sat there like a myth in one of those European paintings, suddenly I was startled to see a deer emerge from the snow. I couldn't believe what I was seeing, as I looked repeatedly before bringing up my gun. When I clicked off the lens cover, the scope was solid water. The deer must have scented the deer on the ground; it was about seventy yards from that and two hundred yards from me, when I could get a glimpse of it through the snow. It seemed like an eternity that I sat and waited as he slowly came closer to me. The truth would probably be between thirty and ninety seconds. I watched as he moved closer. Then I got a look at his rack, and I'm telling you, it was big. He was a huge, huge buck.

Suddenly it turned and looked directly at me. I didn't move, knowing I was well hidden by the big dead spruce at my back and another live spruce behind that. I knew he couldn't see me because I was not silhouetted against the sky.

So I brought up my rifle again with its frozen scope and used the open sights.

I aimed a little over it at about two hundred yards away and pulled the trigger. I couldn't tell whether I had hit it. It just whirled and looked directly at me. I pulled down right on it this time. It spun around and started to run away from me, ran for a short distance, stopped, and turned to stare directly at me. I still don't know how it could have spotted me; perhaps it was those bright yellow pants I wore. As it looked at me, I aimed for its head, dropping the gun about four inches so I would catch him right in the back. I shot and again he took off running. It took me quite a while to get down from that icy stand. Finally I got to the spot where he had been standing at first, but I could see no signs of blood. I *knew* I had hit him at least once. I kept looking and eventually found some bright red blood spots at the point where I had fired the third shot.

By this time the snow was two to three inches deep, and I was trailing him. The blood trail went directly through a bunch of heavy cuttings of branches which had been left. I feared that I would make too much noise going through there, so I back-tracked and went around that bunch of limbs. Ahead of me about 150 yards I could see him standing and looking for me back in the trail. The snow was really coming down so I still couldn't use my wet scope and certainly didn't have time to clean it off. I pulled the gun up and fired four times at him. I couldn't see any flinching so I didn't know whether I had hit him. It took off running once again, and I returned to where I had left the trail to see if I could determine where he was running. I sure didn't want to lose that buck.

The walking was bad because every twig on the ground was ice coated and snapped loudly if I stepped on it. I returned to where I had last seen blood and saw the buck under a very large spruce tree. I went in and started dragging him. I had walked right by it, and it must have doubled back to avoid me. I wiped off the scope and put the covers on, looking through the open sights. He was looking directly at me. I dropped my sight to the base of his neck and shot.

I killed him right there.

I went in and started dragging him out then, suddenly, the horn was loose. The bullet had hit the neck and come out the rack. When it was registered, the Minnesota record book gave it 160 points. I then pulled it out from under the tree. A few days later, when it was weighed officially, it totaled 225 pounds. That's a big deer. After I had cleaned it out, I returned to the first deer, dragging it out so I could pick it up later. Then I returned to our camp. By the time I got there, my brother John had shot a nine-pointer early that morning and had already put it in the back of his pickup and brought it back to camp. Others, including my dad, were there.

We waited until 11:00 when we could return in the ATV to pull out my two deer and put them in the back of my brother's pickup. Ping and Roy said they'd put their tags on the deer and go into town to register them. They got to town at about 11:30 and it was extremely cold; about fifteen degrees. After registering the deer they went into a cafe for a cup of coffee. There were several hunters in the cafe and one said, "What in the world are you old guys doing around here?" Roy replied, "Having coffee. You fellows should be out deer hunting." One said, "There's no deer in this weather." Then Roy told him to go outside and look in the pickup truck. The whole cafe emptied. They couldn't believe these old guys had killed those deer. (Of course, they hadn't.)

Anyway, we got nine deer for eleven hunters on that opening day. And on the last day of the season my brother John and I went back. The snow now was a good ten inches deep. We decided to make a little drive into that stand of mine. I went up in that stand and it was about ten degrees below. John made the drive across that beaver dam and back to me. About halfway through out came another spike buck with a little forky horn in about the same place as the one I had shot first. So I dropped this one, too.

That was the first and only year I shot three bucks, and all out of the same stand, too.

Two years later we had an awful wind that blew down that deer stand, and the new younger trees have grown up so hunting isn't good there anymore. But it surely does bring back memories when I go back there and look at that old spruce tree standing up there with part of a deer stand hanging from it.

BOB FERGUSON
Eagan, Minnesota.

* See *All Hell Broke Loose,* by William H. Hull, 1985.

I Spotted It – My Husband Shot It

My husband had been hunting for deer every evening after work but had seen nothing. It was nearing the end of the season and he hadn't had a shot. One afternoon I came out of the shower and glanced out the patio doors.

As I walked out, I was surprised to see a buck standing in the lake near our shore where we live. I quickly called my husband at work to tell him, but he had already left for home which was about twenty miles away. I then went upstairs, dressed, and kept watching that deer, which, obviously was in no hurry to leave.

So I finished dressing and went out the door away from the lake and waited for my husband. When he drove in, I motioned for him to be quiet. As he stepped out of the truck, I told him about the deer.

He went into the garage, got his gun, loaded it and went around to the back of the house. The deer ran out of the lake and over our neighbor's lawn, which happens to be our daughter and son-in-law's house. He then shot the deer.

The next day our daughter, who is no fan of deer hunting, went out and bought a No Hunting sign and erected it on their property.

IDA MACFARLAND
Pillager, Minnesota

One Shot Didn't Kill This Deer

My brother and another close friend were deer hunting north of Floodwater, Minnesota, where we have a deer shack.

They had parked a new station wagon on the road and had gone into the woods to hunt. They shot an eight-point buck with one shot and decided that since they were only a mile from the shack, they would throw the deer in the back of the station wagon and take it to the shack where it would be easier to dress it out. So they proceeded with that plan.

My brother started the car and had gone only a short distance when he looked in the rear-view mirror and saw the buck's head sticking up, wide awake and looking at them.

My friend thought he should get in the back with the deer to keep it from damaging the inside of the car with its antlers. The deer went wild, started to bleed profusely, while the friend held on. They decided to stop the car, pull the deer out the rear of the wagon, and try to shoot it again.

My brother stopped the car, loaded his gun, and went to the rear of the station wagon to pull out the wildly thrashing animal. It was kicking furiously and bleeding badly.

Just as they started pulling the deer out of the wagon another carful of hunters arrived to watch what was going on. The deer was finally pulled out of the vehicle and quickly stood up. My brother was about to fire the rifle when the deer fell over dead.

The other group of young hunters just about died laughing.

They finally put the dead deer back in the station wagon and returned to the shack.

It took two days of cleaning to get all the blood out of the new station wagon.

PATRICK J. CONLEY
Edina, Minnesota

Meat for the Kids

We live in a small Minnesota town Up North in the Iron Range, that part of the state where iron ore was discovered ages ago and has been mined ever since. We haven't always lived in town actually, but lived twenty miles north, out in the native woods, on a small scrabble farm, where it was so impossible to make a living that we had to move to town for a job, for welfare assistance, and for the future of our family—wife Hilda, two preteen boys, and me, an unemployed miner.

I well remember sitting on the edge of our iron-frame bed early on that winter morning. It was one of those truly great and exhilarating mornings God gave us northerners, when the moon was so brilliant it practically lighted the whole world, when the chimney smoke went straight up into the everlasting sky, when it was so damned cold you wondered how you'd make it through the day.

I had awakened because I was worried about our family, my hungry family which had gone to bed without enough dinner and soon would awaken, hungry, to a house where there was nothing to eat. Well, maybe we still had a couple of those windfall apples we had scrounged from a lone tree in a nearby deserted farmyard.

We were poor and had fought hard to raise food on this hard thin soil. It was so thin and rocky it would support only a few cows while the few calves which came along were quickly killed and devoured by the wolves. So, we couldn't develop even a small herd. We couldn't even make it with chickens either, and the small garden was an impossible dream.

As I sat there with my feet getting dangerously cold, I could only think of venison. "If I could only get a deer," I thought. "It would at least give us some food."

So, I made my decision.

I didn't have a license (who had money for one?) and if I were caught it would be jail for me, but, hells bells, man, when your kids are at the near-starvation level, when your wife is weak and sickly from malnutrition, when your own gut is grumbling for food, you are at the stage where you have to do something.

I dressed quietly, trying to avoid awakening the family, donning heavy wool underwear, a red hunting outfit of pants and jacket, which I'd worn for years, plus part-rubber boots, a heavy hunting cap and wool-lined horsehide mittens called "choppers" (because woodsmen used them all winter to save their fingers).

Then out into the fifteen-below-zero weather, determined to break the law, although I didn't quite think of it in that way. I was the prehistoric meat hunter out to feed his family.

Down beyond the barn I could hear wolves yowling and thought I saw them chase something over the hill, but it wasn't very light yet. I tried to follow them, thinking I might even waste a couple of valuable cartridges to kill a couple of the predators and alleviate their pressure on my diminishing herd. But they were gone.

Our few cattle were quiet inside the shack we called a barn.

There were no cornfield remnants in that area, just natural food for the deer, so I went into the woods to a spot I had seen them bed down, thinking I might have a chance there.

I'd barely reached that area when I jumped a young buck; small horns but tender meat, I thought. He was foolish and stopped running to turn to look at me standing there. The old 30-30 did its job, and I had my deer on the ground.

Now what?

First, the obvious. It had to be gutted and dressed out for health's sake and to lighten the load, which I had to drag a mile or so to the house. Then it had to be butchered into manageable pieces and let freeze in our spare bedroom, which we would use as a freezer.

It was now daylight but extremely cold. Each breath showed up as steam and my sputum froze before it hit the ground. It must be thirty below, I thought.

The family was still asleep as I went into the house to build up the wood fires in a couple of stoves, one being the kitchen cookstove. Also I wanted to get our sturdy kitchen butcher knife, a Shapleigh we had around for many years. Then, outside again.

I was feeling relaxed as I quartered and cut up the venison on an old worktable in the yard. The meat was already freezing rapidly, so I had to move quickly. First, to get some prime cuts for breakfast, then to cut a few steaks, large pieces for pot roasts, plus select pieces for venison stew because that splendid wife of mine, Hilda, could make the world's best stew out of venison. She also made great pasties, those Welsh miners' meat pies, which the women made for the men to take into the mines and to heat over their miners' lamps for a meal.

This meat would be used. Not a drop would be wasted. Every scrap, except some fat, would go for human sustenance.

The kitchen stove was ready, so I put on the large cast-iron skillet and heard the sizzle as the meat hit the pan.

So did my twelve-year-old, Eric, hear it. I heard him pad into the kitchen, barefooted, get a whiff and say, "Dad, you got a deer already this morning! Great!" That made it all worth while for me.

We'd all have full bellies again.

Name withheld on request.
Northern Minnesota, near Canada

Bucks, Brothers, and Boondoggles

A lot of families do it. The scattered are gathered once a year for a family reunion. Our family reunions may have been a bit different in that they were held in a remote area of jackpine country where my wife and I owned forty acres of wild land. We hosted the reunion the third Saturday in September and planned for the November hunt. Some years the weather was hot and other years it was cold and wet, but it didn't seem to matter. We always enjoyed a delicious potluck dinner under a dining fly while discussing events of the past year.

After the noon meal, while the ladies packed the leftovers in ice chests, the kids ran down the mowed path to the frog pond. They delighted in trying to catch a live frog but usually returned with only muddy feet and hands.

We men sat around the campfire if the weather were cold and we were inclined to tell a few stories about the good old days. If the weather was hot, some preferred to sit closer to a beer cooler, but the conversation usually followed the same vein. Eventually someone had to shoot last year's buck just one more time.

My brothers lived in the coulee country of southeast Minnesota, about one hundred miles from our forty. There we hunted weekends, driving out to a place called Hungry Hollow. It was the country where we had been born and raised, so we knew what stump to sit on with a twelve-gauge shotgun across the knees. Some years they were lucky and saw the buck before he saw us. When we were real lucky, we got a close shot and had some venison for the pot.

It was at one of these reunions that we made plans to hunt together on my land, which was in good deer country. The forty was surrounded by thousands of acres of public forest land—and the nine-day season was appealing to us. I had just made a job change and was able to take time off for the entire season. My brothers were both retired. We had waited a long time for this opportunity.

One who has spent any amount of time in a deer camp soon learns to recognize the difference between a cabin and a shack. I owned a shack. A good friend gave me an old woodshed and helped me move it to our forty on a flatbed truck. I later obtained a small log lean-to, and with the aid of a chainsaw and a lot of hard work I mated the two buildings together into a shack that would accommodate four compatible persons overnight. Fresh water was available by priming a pitcher pump mounted on a sand point driven into the ground. There was no electricity; light was provided by a Coleman lantern. A small wood-burning stove provided heat; cooking was done on a two-burner propane stove. Double-deck bunks utilized the lean-to sleeping quarters quite efficiently.

At one time the wind and the mice could pass through the cracks in the walls quite freely. Thanks to some friends, Bill and Bernice, who had used the shack the previous season, the cracks were stuffed with insulation. For some reason, Bernice insisted that all the cracks be plugged before retiring for the night.

Ed, LeRoy, and our brother-in-law, John, arrived at the shack the afternoon before opening day of the gun season. According to our plan, we spent the afternoon scouting the area. I showed them what I thought might be good deer stands. "Don't move from your stand the first weekend," I suggested. "There is fairly heavy hunting here the first two days, so let the deer come to you."

The first day went well. All three saw deer with horns, but LeRoy was the only one of us who dropped a buck. One buck on the meat pole at camp that night seemed to be justification for a picture, so one was taken of the hunter and his kill. His partners displayed a sign at the site which said: "No amount of skill will ever replace dumb luck."

We enjoyed a drink of brandy and had a chili supper. I had volunteered to be the camp cook and willingly accepted compliments on my cooking as the guys took second and third helpings. They failed to realize that my good wife had made the chili the week before and had frozen it, and all I had to do was to thaw it out and heat it. After I had cooked a few meals from scratch, it became apparent to them that I was not the Cajun Chef.

Sunday morning LeRoy and I went to early mass. The service

was quite short, because the padre was wearing his red hunting pants beneath his robe.

It rained hard that Sunday afternoon, so we relaxed at the shack. After all, we mused, we had all week to hunt. That eveing we played some nickle-dime poker. In the midst of the game LeRoy said "Deal me out," grabbed his jacket and took off for the privy in a howling wind.

Time can go fast when the cards are good so I didn't realize that LeRoy had been gone for nearly an hour when I had a horrible thought. The door to the privy had an outside spring-loaded latch. It had never presented any problem because the door was usually left open a bit when the house was in use.

Had the wind blown the door shut? Was LeRoy trapped? My questions was answered by a loud crash like a tree branch falling to the ground. A shivering LeRoy appeared in the doorway, his voice hoarse from hollering for help.

"I fixed your damned door," he muttered.

Fixed indeed! Examination the next day revealed a huge gaping hole in one of the privy panels. After exhausting his lung power, LeRoy had found a three-inch-diameter survey pipe stored in the privy and had used it for a battering ram to break his way out.

And that night we received twelve inches of new snow.

The weekend hunters were gone from the area and the woods were silent. We played "fox and goose" with several deer for the next few days, but the deer were foxier than we were, especially the bucks. We saw nothing with horns. As hunters we were far better fishermen.

Our hunt ended abruptly one evening when a friend showed up to inform us of the death of my brother's friend back home. The next morning I helped them load up a nice buck and bid them farewell. We had enjoyed five unforgettable days together.

Although l have spent many nights alone at my shack in the past, it never seemed as lonely before as it did now.

My enthusiasm for hunting was gone. I loaded my car and snapped the lock on the hunting shack door.

It was then I remembered what an old hunter had once told

me: "Happiness is shooting a deer, for some hunters. To others it is outsmarting a buck. To me it's spending the season in good company, free from the cares of everday life.

Now I know what he meant.

ELMER W. SPRICK
Lake City, Minnesota

My First Deer Hunting Trip – At Age Fifty-Three

It was November 1983 and this was to be my first deer hunting trip, at age fifty-three. My brother, Ray, and friend, Harry, hooked me on deer hunting by preparing a meal of venison while we were on a salmon fishing trip to Lake Michigan earlier that year.

The day before our season began we scouted the area in the southeast corner of the state where they had hunted in prior years and found an appropriate place for my stand. We were staying in Harry's camper truck near a friend's barn.

We were off to a good start with a heavy rain all of Friday night and early Saturday morning. It would have frightened Noah so, instead of going directly to my stand, we poured another cup of coffee and I asked them, "What do I do with the deer after I drop it with my twenty-gauge slug?" They explained how I would have to field dress it by making the appropriate cuts for either a male or a female deer, properly gutting it, and then spreading the rib cage to allow for cooling.

The rain started to let up a bit so I walked the mile to my stand. Approaching it I saw another hunter about fifty yards away, so I stopped to visit with him. He was going to join his group for a drive, so we soon parted. I proceeded to my stand.

In less than an hour I saw a big doe coming up a trail into a wooded area. My heart started pounding at a frantic rhythm that I imagine is familiar to most, if not all, hunters. My first shot was disappointing because it seemed only to turn her away from me, but all was not lost because coming up the same trail about thirty yards behind her was a beautiful buck. But he kept going on the trail and soon came to a wire fence. His brief pause there was to be his last. My slug caused an immediate turn over and quickly all four legs were pointed to the sky.

As I had been instructed by Ray, I stayed where I was and offered a thanksgiving prayer, which took up some of the time I was supposed to wait and watch the deer. Then I huried over to him and found that he was definitely dead.

What a thrill! A twelve-point buck in the first two hours of my hunting experience.

I didn't notice that the rain was starting to come down again, removed my backpack, and took out the knife I had recently purchased at a neighbor's garage sale and performed the appropriate operations. The heart and liver went into the plastic bag I had been told to bring along and were placed in the chest cavity. Then I started dragging that beauty through the woods. I didn't get too far because of the rough terrain, so I stopped to step off the ninety paces from my stand to where I had dropped the deer—and relived the entire event until my brother came by to join in the celebration and to help drag the deer into camp.

The rack is on my home office wall and the front legs form a gun rack, which holds the shotgun I used. I still have the slug which we found when we butchered it. In subsequent years I've had other good shots but haven't been as lucky as that first day. Maybe next season . . . .

WALLY VAVROSKY
Richfield, Minnesota

You Smell Worse Than the Deer – and It's Dead!

We had just come into town from a long weekend hunting out of a gyppo shack just north of Cook, Minnesota. As others have indicated in this book, most deer shacks are pretty basic and have few if any facilities for keeping clean. As a result, we were usually pretty grungy when we came back to civilization.

Tom was rather typical. He never wanted to change underclothing because it was too cold to do so at any given time. Like most of us, he wore rather traditional underwear next to the skin, over which he put woolen long johns as protection against the twenty-below-zero weather we usually encountered. When he finally was warmed up in the shack after a day in and out of a tree stand and much sweating, about all the clothing he was willing to remove would be his outer wools—pants and jacket. The rest he tried to keep on for the cold nights when the stove fire went down or maybe even out. Sometimes he would remove the heavy boots too early before going to bed, walking around in the shack in heavy wool hunting stockings, with cotton undersocks next to the skin to wick away the sweat when it occurred. Then, as he cooled down, his feet darned near froze in the shack, the only solution being to hit the sleeping bag as soon as possible. Of course, while his feet were nearly freezing in the shack, his head and chest were boiling, causing the sweating to continue as if in a Native American sweat lodge. And sometimes he'd hit the brandy bottle a little too hard, trying to relax and get some sleep.

Tom was pretty typical of each of us, even when the weather alleviated (Did it ever alleviate? I don't remember that.) he'd maybe omit a few layers of underwear or wool shirts. Maybe only one pair of choppers (those heavy horsehide mittens with removeable woolen liners, maybe knitted by an elderly relative, like my wife's nonagenarian aunt.

But there were always innovations such as Dick, the second man, made easily. He quickly learned that he could stand the cold better if he slipped a pint of anything alcoholic into his huge jacket pocket when he was heading outside for a day in a tree stand. This only caused one embarrassment, when he went to sleep, fell out of the stand, landed on a tree stump, and broke his arm.

Harry (That's right, Tom, Dick, and Harry) was probably the strongest, best-conditioned one of the bunch. A born winner, he had been a Marine captain, retired. A great admirer of Teddy Roosevelt. He had run his military and civilian life at the panic level, letting his team's daily chores reach the nearly final or near-to-desperation level before taking action. At those times he was apt to say something like "C'mon, guys. Let's get going. Let's take that damned mountain." Or, "Let's get out there and get all of those damned deer so we can go home." Or, "Let's work your asses off so we can meet this new goal and then go celebrate." Harry was a great man, but I always wondered how many men he had killed leading them furiously up that always-present hill. I hated that part of his psyche, or was it psycho? He ruptured himself helping four other fellows lift a 120-pound deer into the back of a pickup. Isn't that improbable? His share of that deer weighed less than 25 pounds.

Bill always admitted that deer hunting was the dirtiest experience he had ever gone through, the dirtiest sport. He found it impossible to wash his hands as much as needed, or his face. In cold water from a lake, no less. We would bring it inside in a bucket, throw a little over our hands, maybe splash a little on our face, howling with imagined pain. Shave? Hot water for a shave? You've got to be kidding or out of your mind to even suggest it.

Of course, someone always brought up the old story. He had supposedly brought along an electric razor, and where was the tree that had been hit by lightning so he could plug in his shaver?

After all the sweaty hours of walking through the woods, overdressed and sweating after climbing up the different trees, some with the legitimate stand therein and some just being one that looked deceptively easy to climb, after sweating for hours in the same clothes from these efforts, during which the tension of looking for a deer, of hearing the little forest noises that all sound like an approaching deer, after the fatigue of a lousy night's kicking around in an undersized sleeping bag, thrown on a hard-board bunk and sweating more during the night—after four days of that experience, any human animal would be ready for hosing off.

Then came the kill. The good fortune of nailing a 225-pound buck, wrestling it over to dress it, getting blood, feces, entrails all over the hunting clothes, manhandling that deer into a vehicle, and riding 250 miles home, overheated and sweating to beat hell.

No wonder when we stopped for coffee en route to Virginia, Minnesota, opened our car doors and two truckers taking a breather in their parked rigs nearby, went into REM sleep. And the truckstop waitresses turned to their boss and said "That's it! We quit!"

No wonder when we got to Virginia where our wives awaited us, insulted by our aroma, warned us away with, "Not in my bed, buster, until you take off those stinking clothes and take a bath."

What the hell! Who cared?

The hell of it is that a succesful hunter still has some of that Adonis self-image in the back of his mind. It's hard for him to re-alize that four days in the shack and the woods has made him an unbearable mess.

If it means washing up in water just above freezing level, at the shack, I'm gonna do it. If it means taking along more under-clothing and changing frequently, like any normal human being would do, I'm gonna do it. I owe that to my family.

No longer will a child or a wife say, "Dad, you smell worse than the deer—and he's dead."

ANONYMOUS
Name reserved to preserve his identity.
Minnesota

The Golden Anniversary of Deer Hunting in Missouri

Carteret A. Alsop, of St. Louis, recently completed fifty years of deer hunting, in recent years using an antique rifle, a 45-70 single-shot breechloader made in 1873. Prior to that he had used a Springfield 30-06, a World War I–vintage rifle known to millions of hunters. He started deer hunting in 1944, which was the beginning of modern deer hunting in Missouri. At that time the Missouri Department of Conservation decided that twenty years of non-hunting was long enough and permitted an opening in twenty counties, legal only for forkhorn bucks and for a two-day season of November 3 and 4. Alsop was invited by a friend, the late Reverend Robert Schwegal, to hunt out of a friend's place on the Meramec River near Meramec State Park in a community of summer houses known locally as Sleepy Valley.

"Neither one of us knew a thing about deer hunting, but we did know that the park had been a refuge that the conservation people had used during the restoration project," said Alsop. "The park," he continued, "had always had deer there and a lot of trapping [was done in the area]."

He commented that neither man even saw a deer the two days they were there.

Admitting that they didn't know how to proceed, he stated that they wandered around, trying to pick a spot. Each time they settled, they'd look around "and there was another hunter glaring at us for crowding in on him."

So they didn't bag a deer that year, but Alsop remembers that the owner of the Hodnut Hotel in Valley Park did score and drove around town with his game on the fender of the car. "Just seeing a deer in those days was a big deal and shooting one was something you just had to tell everybody." Only 583 deer were taken in that 1944 hunt (8 percent), while the 1994 record was expected to reach 155,000 deer for a success rate of about 33 percent. Fifty years made a huge difference!

Having retired as a hospital administrator in 1989, Alsop reminisced. "You couldn't buy ammunition then. In fact," he continued, "Stores didn't have any and one clerk told me that if I had a half dozen rounds it was a lot. Most people went out with three or four rounds and, of course, that was a problem because you were supposed to target your rifle before going hunting." This is west by southwest from St. Louis.

Although Alsop has hunted each of the fifty years since the 1944 opening, he has only bagged three deer. But deer weren't as numerous during those years as they are today. Discussing the scarcety of game of all kinds in the forties, Alsop remembers that it was "[probably] in 1937 or 1938 when I was visiting some friends on a farm near Freeburg. While we were there a neighbor came in and was very excited. What was so unusual as to cause that excitement? He said he'd found the track of a deer."

* "Mr. Alsop lives in St. Louis. This material is drawn from the November 20, 1994, issue of the *St. Louis Post-Dispatch* with the knowledge and permission of editor William Woo.

The Most Incredible Afternoon
I Ever Spent Hunting

October 30, 1994, was not a typical autumn day in Minnesota; it was warm. We don't get to experience many Indian Summer days like this, and I wanted to enjoy it to its fullest. I had spent the morning working around the house performing the usual chores which had to be completed before snow began to fall. The memory of the Halloween blizzard of 1991 was still fresh in my mind, and I had no intention of being caught off guard as I had been that year. It was the Sunday before the firearms deer opener and there was one project I was actually looking forward to doing. I had planned on doing some scouting around my friend's property and hanging my portable tree stand.

My friend Jeff had purchased the property the previous summer and granted me permission to hunt if I so wanted. How could I resist? This land was ten minutes from my home and hadn't been farmed in several years. It was prime deer habitat— the fields had grown over and the pasture grass was at least knee high. There were small pockets of deciduous forest, primarily oak, elm, poplar, and birch trees, along with a large tamarack swamp and several smaller and low areas. The neighboring farmers provided the deer with their choice of corn or alfalfa; this spot provided plenty of cover and security. The idea of filling my freezer with a nice cornfed buck or doe sounded great. I had bowhunted this area once before and had already placed one portable stand but had not seen any deer.

I loaded my car with my bow, tree steps, and my other "portable" stand, which was home made and known by anyone who attempted to carry it as "The Iron Duke." The frame was made of steel; the platform and seat consisted of plywood and conduit. The platform was supported by two cables attached to the frame with turnbuckles. The turnbuckles allowed the platform to be leveled if needed. The whole thing was secured to a tree by a heavy chain. It weighed approximately thirty-five pounds and was extremely awkward and noisy to carry, but it got the job done.

When I arrived I grabbed the "Duke," some tree steps and

started walking. I hadn't much of an opportunity to get to know the land, so I figured I'd spend the afternoon just walking, hiking around to see if I could find a prime spot in which to hang my stand. I wandered around for about an hour and a half until I found the perfect spot; there was a deer trail running between two low areas. It was shaped somewhat like an hourglass with the trail running right through the narrow part of the grass. A medium-sized oak tree stood about ten yards from the trail. The oak wasn't very straight, but I figured I could hang the stand and get it leveled using the turnbuckles.

I started up the tree, screwing in tree steps as I went. The work wasn't difficult but, due to the high temperatures, I worked up a sweat in no time. I placed eight steps, which placed me about fifteen feet off the ground and provided me with a full view of the trail. Then came the nasty part of the job, hauling up the "Iron Duke." I never did get around to installing some kind of a strap to enable me to carry the stand on my back, so it was necessary to hold the stand with one hand while climbing with the other. The stand banged and clanged as I made my way up the tree. It must have sounded like a wrecking yard. I finally made it to the last step and wrapped the chain around the tree, securing it in a fairly level spot. When I attempted to attach the platform cables to the frame, I discovered that both of the turn-buckles had fallen apart while I was walking. There was no way to secure the platform.

In disgust, I unhooked the chain and allowed the stand to crash to the ground. By now I was soaked with sweat and thoroughly fed up. I hauled the "Duke" the half mile back to the car and tossed it into the trunk. I still had some time, so I decided to move my other stand to the new location. This was a store-bought portable which weighed about seven pounds and came with straps allowing me to carry it on my back and easily move it whenever I wished. I retrieved the stand, removed the steps from the tree, and set off to relocate my prime spot. I placed the stand in the tree and spent about twenty minutes cutting shooting lanes so I could use it for bowhunting. After completing the job, I still had about an hour of daylight remaining and was debating whether I should continue bowshooting or get out of the woods and let things quiet down. I thought, Why not hunt; you never know what might happen.

I hurried back to the car to retrieve my bow and settled into my stand with about thirty minutes of hunting time remaining. I didn't really expect to see anything due to the amount of noise I had made in getting set up.

The squirrels immediately started driving me nuts. I kept mistaking their foraging for food in the dried leaves for deer walking through those same woods. I kept thinking I was foolish for hunting after all the noise I had made. I kept recalling all the articles I had read when everything had gone wrong and still the hunt ended successfully.

With only about five minutes of shooting time left, I heard what I thought was another squirrel; I looked to my left and saw a very nice buck walking down the trail. My mind started to race. I kept telling myself: stay calm, take your time, don't misjudge the range, pick your spot, this is one beautiful buck. He was walking down the trail toward my stand and things were looking good. As his head disappeared behind a tree, I drew my bow and waited. He stepped out fom behind the tree, turned his head, and looked directly at me. I froze. I had heard about a deer's ability to jump the string, and I didn't want to take a chance while the buck was watching me.

There is something unnerving about having a big deer stare directly at you from fifteen yards away. He knew there was something different about that tree he was watching, but he couldn't determine what it was. Fortunately, the wind was out of the southwest and he couldn't determine my scent. We were having a staredown. I could see his nostrils flaring as he tried to identify what it was he saw. I was beginning to feel the strain of holding my bow at full draw and was worried that I might not be able to outlast the buck in this test of wills. After what seemed like hours, he must have decided that I was no threat to him so, as he turned to continue down the trail, he offered me a perfect quartering away shot. I took a deep breath, exhaled part of it, aimed, and released.

It looked as if it had been knocked over by a truck. When he attempted to get to his feet, I realized I should knock another arrow in case he tried to get up and run. He attempted to get up several times more, but couldn't. I sat down and waited for the arrow to do its work and couldn't believe this was happening. It was the most exhilirating event I had ever experienced.

The sun was setting and I knew there was no way I was going to drag the deer out by myself, so I rushed home to catch my brother, Tom, before he had picked up his daughter at our house and had gone home. He was still there and went back to help.

All the way he was asking such questions as, "Just how big is it?" How much of antlers? How many points?" I had to tell him I didn't know yet. It turned out to be an eleven-pointer, with an eighteen-inch inside spread. It took Tom and me about forty-five minutes (and approximately ten stops to rest because he was so big) to drag him back to Tom's truck.

I made a few phone calls and did a little bragging. After the calls I took some time to relax. I couldn't believe how physically drained I felt, as if I had just completed a marathon.

And as I said earlier, it was the most incredible afternoon I had ever spent hunting.

Scott P. Reed
Scandia, Minnesota

I Made a Mistake No Deer Hunter Should Ever Make!

My most memorable hunt was in the fall of 1980 near Doris Lake, Minnesota. I was hunting with Sam and Ruth Schmid and their son, Steve, from New Ulm, Bill and Dianne Pruitt of New Ulm, and Joel Fischer from Courtland.

Before we left for the northwoods, instead of borrowing my uncle's 30-30, I bought a used Winchester 30-30 from an elderly gentleman, Alvin Nelson of Lafayette.

"Gun, case, shells, everything goes," he said. I paid Alvin and as I was leaving he stated that it was a "buck rifle. All I ever shot with it were bucks," he said. Just what I needed because I'd been hunting for seven years and had never seen a buck, much less get a chance to shoot at one.

The morning was warm and sunny, and I made a mistake that no deer hunter or anyone entering the woods should ever make. I did not take my compass because I had left it on other hunting clothes; I used the sun for direction as I entered the woods. I used landmarks to guide me. First, an old tree stand, then a slough, and across the slough an old tree, etc.

I sat down to rest in the warm sun and fell asleep. I awoke to a cold chill with heavy snow falling. My sun was gone, my landmarks were gone. I had lost all sense of direction.

I was lost.

I never felt so helpless in all my life. I did not know in which direction to start walking. I started walking and whistling until I heard a faint whistle and found Sam and we headed back to the truck. Ruth, Dianne, and Steve were already there, and the two women stated that they had just seen two does cross the logging road just a short distance away. We all decided to go and take a look but it was still snowing and there was no way I was going back into those woods. Ruth and Dianne were showing Sam and Steve where the does had crossed when I turned around to head back to the logging road; then I came face to face with a nice buck with his nose on the ground coming directly toward me.

I raised my rifle, the buck raised his head, and I shot. This eight-point whitetail was only about twenty-five feet away from me when I shot.

It turned out to be the biggest buck I ever got out of Minnesota's northwoods.

On this trip I learned a lot. I found out how important a compass is and that there really are "buck rifles." It was a good trip for me.

PAUL GUGGISBERG
Lafayette, Minnesota

A Summer in the North Woods in 1907

During my freshman and sophomore years of college, I had a part-time job working in the dairy division on the St. Paul campus, College of Agriculture. This job included sampling and testing the milk of fourteen cows night and morning and teaching milk and the process of buttermaking to the students in the School of Agriculture. Also, I would deliver both cream and butter in St. Anthony Park to members of the faculty and others each Saturday afternoon, using the station-owned horse and buggy.

At the end of my sophomore year, Professor T. L. Haecker, head of the dairy division, told me I should apply for a job as a buttermaker's helper in a cooperative creamery during the summer months and learn the buttermaking trade. I asked what the pay would be and what board and room would cost. The professor thought the pay perhaps would be $20 a month and the room and board about the same.

Since I was working my way through school, that hardly seemed a practical move, particularly since I had no intention of being a buttermaker. The very next day, Dillion Tierney, a forestry graduate, asked me if I would be interested in spending the summer with him in a timber survey in the northwoods. He had been engaged by the Fredrick Weyerhaeuser lumber company to make a scientific check of the timber cruiser's estimates.

The pay would be $50 a month and board. I asked how he could pay that much for a summer vacation in the northwoods. Of course, I said, I'd like a job like that. Dillion said he had also engaged a neighbor's son, Puck.

The very next day we took a train for Carlton, Minnesota, and walked about ten miles to Percy Vibert's[1] cabin. Here we set up camp and dug a hole under the northeast corner of the cabin, that hole to be the cooler for butter, etc. Vibert was not there when we arrived, but he came in before we left.

Tierney was to make a careful check of the timber cruiser's estimates. He had a tool with which he could measure the height of the trees by triangularization. Puck and I had calipers with which we measured the diameters of the trees at breast height.

We also had scratching rods to mark the trees we had measured. These tools had been made by a blacksmith from an old wagon wheel rim.

Our clothing consisted of underwear, a cambric and a flannel, shirt, shagged overalls (i.e., having a rough nap), high-topped shoes, and a felt hat.

This was to be an accurate check of the cruiser's estimates. To the best of my memory, included were white, red and jack pine, spruce, and tamarack.

Vibert's cabin was about ten miles southeast of Carlton. There was an old well-worn Indian trail with brush and small trees on each side. It was called "The Old Sitting Bull Trail," but whether Sitting Bull's squaw ever put up a birch bark teepee there may be questioned. As I walked the ten miles to Carlton on a Saturday night to get our mail, if any, and back after dark, I thought of Sitting Bull and his braves on the warpath.

While we were camped at Vibert's we took a Sunday fishing trip to Twin Lakes and spent most of the day fishing, without much luck. A heavy squall hit while we were still on the lake, and I don't remember whether we caught any fish.

It took us about a month to clean up the work around Vibert's camp, after which we moved to the Cloquet area.

Somewhere along the way we came upon an area where we learned a party of wealthy sports from Chicago had a very elaborate cabin. While on the survey near this location we found five decaying carcasses of deer, each in a different area. The loins and a few other juicy cuts had been used and the rest left to rot.

We had a rifle in camp, but on no occasion did we ever use it, although fresh meat would have tasted very good. As I recall, all the fresh meat we ever had were two or three spruce hens. I got one with a handgun, holding the sight about four inches high, and Puck got one by throwing a piece of iron at it. Later, this technique was called "chunking."

We were working around Cloquet in July and took in the Fourth of July celebration there. The logrolling contest was a favorite among the loggers. We saw a magnificent contest among the best of these logrollers. It was a sport of such agility and balance it must have required a lot of experience and practice. The champion pair jumped and twisted on the whirling log, quickly changing the direction of the whirl to try to dunk the opponent. This particular contest continued for more than an hour, ending when the loser was finally dumped into the lake.

During the foot races Dillion, the hundred-yard-dash man, won in ten seconds flat and the $10 prize. I managed second in the quarter mile and won $5.

While at Cloquet I visited with my uncle, John McNelly. He was a number one timber cruiser and one which Weyerhaeuser took west to Washington state, where they had large timber interests. When I was with him in Cloquet he was scaling the pine logs as they were being dragged from the river to the mill.

Later, Leslie R. Beatty, writing in a forest ranger diary, wrote of the fires of 1922 saying, "Later that day Ranger Vibert[2] and I took off by car from Duluth where we met the first fire crews. For the first time in history an airplane was used (for fire watch). The plane, based at a temporary landing just north of Pike Lake, was piloted by Captain Williams of the Minnesota National Guard. His observer was John H. McNally[3] a top ranking timber cruiser employed by the Cloquet company. McNally knew that area so well that his map revealed nearly the exact edges of the fire and it was of great assistance to us in rescuing the fire crews." (From *Minnesota Conservation*.)

Somewhere on our travels that summer of 1907 we visited what was most typical of the sawmill areas of that time. We saw great pine logs being hoisted to the saws. The sweet odor of pine lumber filled the air. This was a city of rough-sawed lumber, at least thirty or forty trees being piled in orderly fashion around the area. The pungent odor of pine was everywhere. Dillion found the clerk in a building of rough-sawed lumber and had a good long talk with him.

There were ups and downs on the trail. There seemed to be a seasonal distribution of nasty insects and pests. We never did get them under control. We tried mosquito repellents without much success. They swarmed around us by the thousands. We tied red bandana handkerchiefs around our heads and necks, and still they seemed to be eating us up. After the mosquitoes came the gnats—the "Bite-ums, no see-ums"—followed by the black flies. These did not bite but just buzzed around us all day long.

We, of course, used spruce boughs for our beds. We spread mosquito bar on "Y" sticks in the ground for night cover, but this didn't work too well. Finally we were able to get cheesecloth, which was woven finer and was a great help, but at night the bugs would fly in while we were getting under the covers. Tierney would light a match and kill them one at a time. Puck and I probably got more bites.

One day when we were going down a trail I smelled wood smoke and said, "There's a logging camp ahead." Sure enough, and with a lonely caretaker in charge. He was glad to see us to have somone to talk with. It was about noon and we had to stay for dinner, which we did gladly. We had sour dough bread, tea, baked beans, and prunes.

Later we cleaned up on an area of timber and then hiked twelve miles through small but thick timber growth and came out at the end of a logging road at Orr. We weighed in there and the packsack weighed ninety-six pounds.

It was noon and we were invited to eat at the road camp. We were naturally hungry for the camp food after living on oatmeal and burned bread dough. Puck and I really filled up on the camp food that was set before us. This included generous servings of beef. This was a Friday and Puck and I felt sorry for Dillion who could not eat meat on Friday. I don't recall that we talked about it except to express our sorrow for him. We noticed a slight taint to the beef, but we were hungry so we helped ourselves most liberally. After eating we headed for Pelican Lake. It wasn't long before some fast-moving black clouds blocked out the sun, and soon there was lightning and the roll of thunder followed by gusts of cold air. Heavy drops of rain soon became a steady downpour.

We decided to make a quick camp under a giant pine. Puck and I were sick as dogs with ptomaine poisoning, and we spent most of the night out in the wet brush. Puck went in one direction, while I was coming back from the other.

We each made five or six trips out in that downpour. Dillion said, "That was one time my religion paid off."

It was at either Ash Lake or Orr that Tierney bought two birch bark canoes from the Sioux Indians for $10 each. We still had 100 miles to paddle down to the Pelican and Vermillion Rivers, and this was going to turn out to be the most interesting and exciting part of our trip.

We now had a new man, a forestry student from Massachusetts State college; I was given one of the canoes with him in the bow and me in the stern. I showed him how to feather the paddle, but he persisted in jerking the bow sideways. Finally I got mad and told him we would go ashore and fight it out—and only then did he suddenly get the idea, and we finally got moving.

The eastern forestry student, whom I will call Sam, was apparently raised in the city and seemed to have little originality and no ambition. He had never been in fast water. He found fault with the grub and the way it was cooked, but refused to do any cooking himself. On one occasion when Dillion was blazing out an eighty line, Sam and I had crossed a trail without seeing a corner where we should have turned. After walking some distance, I decided we had missed the turn and we started back. Sam was getting madder and madder at me for missing the turn, but when we got back he was so bewildered that he started running down the cross trail in the wrong direction. I called and told him so, but he kept going—hollering at the top of his voice. I went ahead and told Dillion what had happened. He said Sam would get lost for sure so started out after him, soon catching him and straightening him out. Sam left for home soon after that, having spent less than a month in the timber.

It was necessary to keep the canoes in shape and at nearly every stop we'd caulk the leaks with spruce gum. As we neared one of the rapids, Dillion asked me to portage my canoe while he shot the rapids.

Several times while working in marshy areas we would come on beauitful wild gardens of Indian moccasins, both pink and yellow, and often blue flags and other beautiful wildflowers. In the hot summer we could use our hats to dip up cold water from among the roots of the tamarack trees.

One day we came across a log cabin where timber cruisers had staked out the corners of a quarter section and cleared enough land for a potato patch. It must have been August since the potatoes were of some size. We gathered a mess and roasted them in our campfire ashes that night for a nice variation in our diet. We felt sure that the squatter was a hospitable fellow and would want us to do this.

Somewhere along our journey, which I can't locate now, we ran across a logging camp with thirty or forty piles of rough-sawed pine boards drying on a fine summer day. I shall never forget the sweet scent of that newly sawed lumber.

There was a young clerk who had an office of this rough-sawed pine; we visited with him for some time and Dillion had a good logging talk with him. He seemed to have the duties of both clerk and watchman.

As we went along, we would occassionally take a swim in a lake or river. There had been some heavy rains, and the Vermillion river was out of its banks in some places. One cool night when we had tented on the shore I thought I would walk out in the fairly shallow water and take a quick bath. Before I knew what had happened I was under the rushing water. That was one time I was glad I could swim.

We soon portaged our last rapids. Our grub was gone. The last three days we had only oatmeal and sugar to eat and were glad to have that. However, when we reached the fishing camp at the mouth of the Vermillion river, where it empties into Lake Vermillion, our breakfast consisted of three eggs each and all the flapjacks we could eat.

We took the lake boat to Tower, where we put up at a hotel for the night. Dillion and Puck were unfortunate enough to have a bed recently vacated by lumberjacks and were affected with "gray backs" (lice) during the night. I was lucky to have a clean bed. We had played poker with matches for plunder. Needless to say, no one got rich before we finished the job. The cards were so worn and marked that we could read most of them from the backs.

I came out of the trip with one much-worn shirt, the shagged-off pants were worn-out, while the high, pegged shoes were about as good as new. The hat was gone.

We took the train from Tower to Duluth the next morning. I went directly from Duluth to Madison, Wisconsin, where I enrolled as a junior in the Wisconsin college of agriculture. Puck went back to high school and Dillion took another assignment.

Puck became cashier in the home bank. He died relatively young. I finished a good year at the University of Wisconsin and took a ten-month job on a cost-accounting route at Northfield, once again came in second in a Fourth of July foot race at Dundee. While on the Northfield route, I saw presidential candidate William Taft ride an elephant in the Rice county fair, heard Chauncy Alcott sing, and also met my future wife.

C. L. McNelly (deceased 1977)
as told to son R. K. McNelly
Edina, Minnesota

1. The author spelled this name both Vibert and Vifert.

2. Ibid

3. Again, confusion. It is unclear to editor Hull that the source quoted in C. L. McNelly's notes was unintentionally misspelled as being McNally, perhaps by a typist long ago.

A Footrace with a Deer

Of my many deer hunts, one stands particularly high on my list. It happened here on my own place in central Minnesota. My son, Terry Marshall, Don Block, and Craig Ceriuym, sons-in-law, were to hunt the 240 acres of fine timber north of our farm buildings. Craig and I took stands on the north end, Craig taking his on the open country on the northeast, while I chose a site in the timber close to a creek bordered by heavy brush.

We were alerted by a shot in the area where the boys had started driving. A large buck came by heading into the drive. At the time of my shot I could see he was hit. Soon he appeared again on a low hill, as if he were trying to lie down. It was obvious he was having trouble doing so. I took a few shots, but he disappeared. I slipped another shell into the gun and headed for where I had last seen him.

Before I got to him, he got up from the grass and started running; I took a shot and missed. Having no more shells in my gun I started running after him. I was easily able to keep up with him and my main thought was to keep him from getting into the brush where I'd probably lose him. So Don came to me, and then there were the three of us running together, two men and the deer.

After running for some time, Don said, "You'd better shoot him or he'll get away." Embarassed, I said, "I have no more shells." I know he was embarrassed to have to shoot my deer and also to think that he, a good shot, had to kill a cripple. Then I checked my gun and I was more embarrassed than he was.

I still had one live shell in my gun.

Soon the other boy came and one went down to the building to get a tractor and a wagon. My daughter, Sally, came back with the wagon. Soon we had the buck loaded and Terry spoke up.

Terry said he would walk back through the timber because he had gotten that first shot at a deer which came through the drive. Sally was standing in the wagon watching Terry leave. She saw him raise his gun and shots rang out. We then had another buck, with only a short drag to the wagon.

111

I still have those heavy antlers hanging on the wall to remind me of a very pleasant hunt.

There was still a fly in the ointment. Don always had this to hang on me and keep me in his place. I was the man who would rather run his deer down on foot than count the shells in his gun. There is the old saying about catching someone with his pants down and about that time I said there would come a time when I would catch Don with his pants down.

Little did I know how soon that prophesy would be fulfilled.

To have eaten a piece of my mother's or my wife's cake was a great experience. To have eaten it with their favorite frosting was even better. This I compare to having hunted in our own state versus hunting in another one, too.

We had eaten our cake, but now how about the frosting?

Why not Wyoming?

Terry located a large ranch near Douglas, Wyoming, where we could hunt, but lodged in Douglas. The chance of hunting was thrilling so we drove most of the night. No one complained. We were there in time to look over the ranch before opening day. The ranch was large, made up of smaller holdings, some still having buildings thereon. The rancher set up an office where his hunters all met on opening day and where we were assigned hunting areas. Our area was quite far back and had fewer antelope. The deal was that if we hadn't any luck by noon, we should return and if the hunters across the railroad tracks had gotten theirs we could hunt there. The rancher was careful to avoid having too many hunters in one area at the same time.

On the way out we saw a buck standing on a hill. To avoid alerting him we slowed down and Don rolled out; we drove on and stopped, heard a shot, went back, and loaded up his buck.

Having never hunted antelope before, I made the mistake of watching from a hilltop. The antelope were always out of range. I would have been better off hunting from a trail—and much less conspicuous. A large buck came my way soon, and I thought I couldn't hit him by shooting from a standing position, so I'd try a prone position, but there was no place the cactus would let me get prone.

I heard a shot from the direction Terry had gone so decided to go to him. He had a nice buck. Then I took off to find the other boys. Going around a small hill, I saw a sight that gladdened my heart. Here was Don with his pants down and Terry was picking cactus thorns out of his leg. We were even now, but how long would that last?

Jim had gotten his antelope by then so we decided to try our luck on the other side of the railroad tracks. Lo and behold, just as we got to the tracks, there was a buck running up the tracks. Someone said, "Shoot," but someone else said, "You can't! That's railroad property." When someone said, "There are no signs," I uncased my gun and reached into my pocket for shells, coming up with a box of cough drops. I'm sure my performance would have been appropriate material for an old Laurel and Hardy movie. Who cared? We had our antelope.

The boys did invite me to go hunting with them again, so I suppose they thought it all right to hunt with a clown, providing he's a lucky one.

We had some time left so we had the privilege of enjoying many of the sights of the glamorous old West.

Our trip back home brought us one small accident. Just as we were passing an oncoming car, three deer ran between us. It was incredible that only one got hit. It seemed like a rag when the car hit it and tossed it aside, with no harm to the vehicles.

JOHN MARSHALL
Verndale, Minnesota

Frank Faces the End of His Hunting Years

Clair Dziuk, my dad, and his brother-in-law, Frank Kozisek, were a couple of deer hunters from Foley, Minnesota. They began to hunt together in the mid-thirties and after about 1960 hunted from a shack north of Duluth with other family members. Clair had been born in 1907 and Frank earlier, in 1895, so they were getting along in years.

One day in the early 1980s they were hunting and met in the woods about midday. The younger man, Clair, said he felt dizzy and had a headache; he was also somewhat disoriented. Frank admitted that he had the same problem, the same symptoms, so they sat down on a windfall to discuss what it could be. Did they both have the flu or some botulism from something they had eaten? Clair took his glasses off to wipe away the tears with his big red handkerchief. Frank stared at the glasses as they rested in Clair's hand and said "By golly, Clair, you've got my glasses there." Clair was startled, but looked searchingly at Frank. "And you've got mine!" They switched glasses and their vague illnesses disappeared.

As they grew older, Frank became too feeble to hunt. As he passed the eighty-year mark, not only too feeble to hunt or even go along and stay in the shack, both men felt the shack was too remote in case medical attention was needed. One morning during their last hunting season together, Clair first realized the jig was up and that it was time to gather Frank and get back to civilization. For one thing, Frank hadn't shot a deer for several years, but even though he still loved the season, it was time to call it quits. Clair got the pickup ready, loaded to leave early one beautiful, frosty morning, and helped Frank into the truck. As the headlights picked up various scenes in the vicinity, Clair felt increasingly nostalgic and sentimental. Because both men were very deaf, they always had to scream at each other to be heard. As they wended their way out of the woods Frank said, "Clair!" That was all.

As Clair waited for Frank to continue, Frank again said, "Clair!" speaking even louder this time. Frank half turned to lean closer to Clair, who thought, "Oh, no. Here comes the tears. He's going to cry." Frank realized that Clair was fighting an emotional outburst which was becoming humorous instead of painful. He began to choke up himself. Frank reached out and punched Clair on the arm, a funny little grin on his face, when he said, "Clair, them deer can just kiss my ass."

CLAIR WADE
Foley, Minnesota

My Grunt Call Kept This Buck Coming Back

It was in the fall of 1991 and I had just reached home from college at about 3:00 P.M. As soon as I came in the door, I called my hunting buddy to see if he was going to join me this evening for bow hunting the whitetails. He said he would, so I told him I'd be out in about forty-five minutes to pick him up. I got my things ready to go and was on my way quickly. He was ready to go, so in no time at all we were walking toward our bow stands.

It was in October and the first few traces of snow were already on the ground. I sat for the first two or two-and-a-half hours waiting for the first sign of anything to show. As my hopes were growing dim, I thought it was going to be another uneventful night. Then, as the sun was starting to go down, I could hear the faint sound of a deer walking through the cold, crunchy leaves. I could catch only a glimpse of it walking through the woods about a hundred yards away. But when it stepped out of the woods about eighty yards away I couldn't believe it. It was at least an eight-pointer, but it looked more like a ten.

The first thing he did was to look in my direction, then turned and walked away—in the opposite direction. As he was walking away, I grabbed my grunt tube from around my neck and gave it a soft blow. The buck stopped, looked back at me, and just stood there. After about five seconds more, I gave it another soft blow. That motivated him because he turned and started running right toward me. I couldn't believe it. It was a perfectly symmetrical ten-pointer in about the 120-inch class.

He was now standing in the middle of a field twenty to twenty-five yards away from me. I drew my PSE bow back and put the twenty-yard pin behind his shoulder, and let one fly. The deer bolted briefly and then stopped about fifty yards from me. He just stood there and looked around while I couldn't believe what was going on. I just waited for him to fall, or to do something, so I grabbed my grunt and gave it another gentle blow. He didn't think twice and was quickly standing just where I missed him before. Once again I drew my bow, this time putting the twenty-yard pin on him higher than I had done before.

I let the arrow fly. This time he took off and then just stood there in the field. Now I'm really thinking, "What the heck is going on?" I notched another arrow and gave my grunt a blow. He wheeled around and came running back but this time he was stomping his feet looking like he was ready for a fight. It's hard to explain but I could tell he was looking for the impostor buck.

I drew back, this time putting my thirty-yard pin on him. I let this one fly and, yes, you guessed it, I missed again. Believe it or not, once again he ran away about fifty yards and looked around. By now I was downright ticked off. Notching another arrow, I gave my grunt another blow and here he came right back in again. This time I decided not to use my pins, but drew my bow back to see how the trajectory of the arrow looked. I remember thinking to myself, "Ya, it looks good right there," so I put my head back on my normal anchor point and released. Suddenly I heard and felt the darnedest commotion. It turned out that my grunt tube got interlocked with my bow string. When I released the arrow I saw pieces go flying everywhere, and I about got yanked out of the stand. Believe it or not this buck that would have looked so good on my wall, once again ran only fifty yards, stood there, and looked around. It was almost as if he were waiting for a call from the other buck but, since it didn't happen, he just put his head down and waited.

I'm not at all proud to be the one to tell this story but this little episode with that buck taught me something I could never learn from another hunter.

This isn't a story that I like to tell everyone but I thought it might be neat to have a chance of having an experience that happened to me published. One of the only reasons I ever tell anyone this story is because my buddy, who was out with me, was sitting across the field and saw the whole thing.

CHRIS BUSHINGER
Wadena, Minnesota

The Georgeville Storm

He peered through the window at the swirling snow. He had an uneasy feeling as he heard the wind blow. They readied themselves in the usual way, of a northwoods deer camp on opening day.

Six inches were down as they skidded across the Swan* and then they were swallowed, by the dark of predawn.

Marsh headed west, according to plan; he'd thought this was his year, with his new gun in hand. Three tracks in the snow, two runners behind, Old Jer towed the new sled for the very first time.

They split off for their stands, one by one, first George, then Mic, cradling their guns.

They nodded in silence and gave the thumbs-up sign, then melted away, deep into the pines.

Each hoped for the other, yet prayed for his own chance at the Big One, a chance to atone. Atone for the missed shots or mistakes of the past, the slate would be clean, it was Opening at last. Steam rolled from Jer's shirt as he thought to himself, "This old buck hunter's ready. I'm back down off the shelf."

He stood for a moment, in the enveloping snow, then glanced over his shoulder at the new sled in tow.

He stared at the sled, oak, strong and sleek. It would bring home his game, horns, hide, and meat. From a recurring dream, its design had taken shape, this white oak wonder, this deer-dragging crate.

Twenty-eight hunts had long come and gone. Twenty-nine was upon him at the first breath of dawn. He felt a strange affection for this newfound thing, like an old knife or a familiar ring.

It had moved! He wondered how? Why? Then the spell was broken when he blinked his eye . . . he must press on.

It glided behind him through the deepening snow; he could see the stand now, just a short way to go.

The sled was stashed at the big blow-down, he climbed up the tree, it was time for the showdown.

Late, gray dawn finally broke. The storm raged, an icy fire, freshly stoked. Eight inches by eight, ten inches by ten. By two o'clock eighteen inches of snow had settled in.

In the face of the hunter spewed a freezing grit, but J. T. held steady, he just couldn't quit.

Once again he stared at the runners of that sled and memories of bucks, long ago dead, came alive in his dreams and danced in his head.

Once more he thought he saw movement down there, where the sled lay waiting in the sharp frigid air. The buck rose from his bed when the wind went down, shook the snow from his antlers, he must now make his rounds. From down deep in the cedars he ambled up hill where J. T. and the sled were, silent and still.

By four o'clock, all hands save one, were nestled in camp, on the banks of the Swan. Nervous looks flew from one man to another. They became more worried about their buck-hunting brother.

Toward the hunter he drifted, in snow past his knees, big rack in the air, nose testing the breeze.

The hunter now knew that he'd waited too long, when the feeling in his feet had finally gone. Trying to climb down from his frozen perch, he saw steam from two nostrils by the big yellow birch.

With his ebbing strength he brought the scope to his eye, squeezed the trigger on time, then the great buck died.

Too cold to climb down, he just fell from the tree and struggled to stand on his now-frozen feet. But when he crawled to the kill, he found with surprise that his new oak sled lay by the fallen buck's side.

The knife slipped from his fingers, now frozen like wood; he'd dress him out later, or maybe Mic would. Then with his last ounce of strength and one thought in his head, he rolled that wide-racked buck right onto the sled.

He thought to himself of what the boys might say, about him hunting so long in the storm that day; and when they lay him down, in the cold, cold ground, they'd tip their caps in honor, cause he'd fought his last round.

As he grew weary and colder and stumbled for time, the meat wagon followed with strength of its own! When the twisting Swan River finally came into view, he wished for two things, a brew and a chew.

He looked at his quarry, now still, on the sled, then fell down on the beast, his hands gripped to its head. So close, yet so far. Is it here that I'll die? he thought. I'll just rest for a minute, then he closed his eyes.

Back in Camp Georgeville, after the great storm's wrath, the three lonely hunters wrote Jer's epitaph:

"Somewhere out there old Jer went down
his gun and his body were never found."

The hour slipped by and the fire burned down, then a rumble was felt all throughout Georgetown. And with a final crash, a bump and a roar, buck, sled and hunter broke through the door!

They pried his stiff fingers from the horns of that buck. He'd had the best and the worst of one man's luck.

Rock hard and frozen like a freezer-burned fish, in his teeth was a note like a final last wish. Don't mourn for long, boys, for there's more hunts to come. Just place a three-fingered pinch 'tween my cheek and my gum.

With tears in their eyes, the boys nodded and knew, for the old buck man, it was the least they could do. When they pried his lip open and poured in the Cope, George saw Jer's eye twitch. There still might be hope.

He quivered and shook but couldn't quite wake, yet there might be one chance if it weren't too late. So they turned out the lights and put Marsh, the loudest snorer, to bed, and within moments it worked, he woke up the dead.

They gave Jer a Bud and pinch or three, then they all walked outside for a final look see. The storm had now ended so they looked at the ground, the tracks that they saw were strangely profound.

No footprints around, of any kind, just a laden down sled track, two runners in line.

Now the years have passed, but the boys can't stop bragging, 'bout how old Jer was saved, by the Georgeville meat wagon.

JERRY TRIDEN
Marine on St. Croix, Minnesota

* Editor's notes: Georgeville is the hunting camp named after the owner, George. It's on the Swan river in north central Minnesota.

How to Get Lost in the Woods

Let me tell you of my first day in the woods. Perhaps to begin with, you should know that there were three basic areas where we hunted in the woods at Lake Christine. There was the area basically east of the lake and north of the road. It was a relatively small area, bordered by the lake on the west, the road from the north shore of Lake Superior on the south, a much-used tote road a half-mile east of the lake, and open to the wilderness to the north. The Poplar river flowed south out of the lake. The second area we had dubbed the Big Bend, a larger area south of the road from the north shore, where the Poplar river circled for a mile or so in a big bend. The third area was the area in which the cabin was located on the west side of the lake, bordered on the north by the Sawbill road and without borders on the west and the south. Our party had these areas almost exclusively in those days.

Rarely did we see anyone else there. When we did, the guy was agitated, usually hot (even on the coldest day), scared, red-faced, and his first words were almost always "How do I get out of here?" I had several such conversations with strangers when the conversation started in the same way. When you gave him directions, he was off at a run, never to be seen again. It was our country. You needed to have a rough idea of where you were, and a lot of faith in your compass.

Ernie Raymond took me out for my first day of hunting at this shack; I was seventeen. He assigned me a fine spot near a northbound tote road, near the Poplar river bridge. It was quite open and it looked impossible to get lost in that area. The road at this point was reduced to a well-defined track and there were a couple of frequently used deer trails crossing that tote road, which was a deer trail in itself. Ernie pointed all of this out to me, helped me find a downed tree which was down-wind, where I had a good view of the crossings. Before he left he urged me to keep as quiet as possible and to keep my eyes open, scanning constantly. If I did all of this, he thought I would probably get my deer.

I sat there, gun in lap, getting colder and colder, for about fifteen minutes, rather scared, when I thought I heard a twig break just behind me. I looked over my right shoulder and saw them — a buck and a doe standing not twenty feet from me, watching me, a curiosity in these parts. As I whirled to my left to get lined up for a shot, they spun and were only a pair of white flags by the time I could get them in my sights, the safety off, and my finger on the trigger. How exciting! I was a hunter and there were deer to be conquered.

I sat there until eleven or so, colder and colder, and getting hungry, I ate my lunch — a cold apple and a frozen bitter chocolate bar. I walked up and down the tote road to get warm, went back to my stand where I sat until nearly four o'clock. There were quite a few birds and some small animals, mainly squirrels; I even saw my first ermine, pure white and staring right at me from not more than fifteen feet. I guessed that he wondered what that big creature was doing in his woods. Suddenly I thought I saw something moving directly ahead. I did and it was colored tan. It moved away behind some spruce trees. Of course, I had my gun up, ready, but I couldn't see enough to shoot. The next time I saw it, the head and neck were framed in spruce branches. I fired, aiming where I thought the jugular would be. It dropped immediately. I ran to it but, when it kept kicking its feet, I visualized it rearing up and cutting me with those sharp front hooves. I knew they could be very dangerous since they are known to have gouged hunters seriously. So I stood back and let it have one in the head. It stopped kicking shortly. Later I realized that I had seen a reaction that would have stopped shortly anyhow.

Never had I dressed out anything larger than a squirrel but figured it had to be about the same, so I started the job. Halfway through I realized the sun had gone down and it was getting dark. I began to work frantically, finished in a hurry, locked my license tag on its leg and was ready to start dragging it down the tote road. Stopping to think, I realized I would have a hard time getting it out in the dark, so I covered it with snow and left it there, taking off at a fast clip. It was very dark, there was no moon and, as I hurried, I missed a sharp turn in the trail and soon was fighting underbrush. I soon realized that it was so dark I probably wouldn't know the trail if I got back to it, but knowing the lake had to be a few feet to my right, I opted to go in that direction, and directly across the lake was our cabin. Clear sailing from the shore on. Soon I found the shore but it was at the point where the Poplar river exits from the lake. At that point there were a lot of reeds and a lot of snow at the water line.

I was getting rather desperate to get out of there and suddenly where I walked caved in and I was in the lake almost to my waist. I very quickly reversed my direction back to the shore, which was difficult partly because I was soaked on the lower half, and scared. I stopped to reconsider and heard the babble of the river only fifty feet away. I had gone out on the lake on a sandbar created by the flow of the river. That's what saved me from a serious dunking. I really wasn't in the lake proper.

I started downriver as fast as I could, which was actually very slow, because there was the usual heavy undergrowth along the bank and I didn't dare go far enough away from the river where I couldn't hear the river. It would be no more than a quarter of a mile to the road, but it was tough going, and I knew the others would be worrying about their newest member, me. Sure enough, I soon heard three rifle shots in close succession, the universal emergency signal, directly ahead of me. I answered with a couple of shots in the air and they replied with three more. I was still fighting brush, but it wasn't long before I broke out and saw Dad and a few others standing on the bridge. Others had gone in on the tote road to look for me, but Dad said not to worry. They would have heard our shots and would be along shortly. We headed for the camp in Dad's car. They had been prepared to spend a lot of time to find me, and that surely made me feel good.

The grub was delicious that night, but the gang was quiet. I was reflective and thankful that Ernie had taken me to a stand which wasn't more remote than I could handle. I think everyone was happy that it was as easy as it was on all of us.

After a few years the cabin became too disreputable even for us. Unsafe would be the word. Pop considered it, found he could obtain a ninety-nine year lease on an acre nearby, for a dollar a year. The acre for which he bargained was directly across the road from Mr. Clinch's property, which he had been so kind to let us use all those years. The leasing arrangement changed a few years later, and Dad was able to purchase the acre outright. But by that time we had built the new cabin and were in much better quarters.

R. K. McNelly, Sr.
Edina, Minnesota

As a Photographer I Can Help You Deer Hunt

It felt good to straighten up my back, after hunching over for nearly a half hour to watch for the deer. Trying to move as little as possible while the buck stared at me through the trees was a strain. Now he's gone, just disappeared in the very brush from which he had just emerged moments before.

You see, I'm a different kind of a hunter. For example, I don't even have a scope on my rifle. In fact, I don't even have a rifle. What I do have is a telephoto lens on my 35mm single lens reflex camera.

I'm hunting images, not meat. I'm a photographer.

I'm hunting for perfect photos of deer, of interesting shots that show I have communed with this wild animal, that I have intruded into his home and have captured his very essence in a much more personal way than if I had just wiped out his life. My kind of hunting leaves him ready for you, the game artist, while I may have made him a little more wary of you, a little more suspicious of that unknown shape in the trees.

I had heard the subtle noises he makes as he browsed in the thick brush, inching in my direction. I sat ready behind the camera, checking exposure and focusing on where he might appear. Just as you must anticipate the brush, or trees, or other objects which may distract your game or alert it to your presence, I have to be ready, too. I must think about where the sun will be coming from, its possible intensity and appropriate exposures for a good picture. Like you, I must be sure I don't startle him just before I'm going to shoot the picture. We both must be good still-hunters.

Suddenly, silently, he stepped into view, standing frozen, listening for danger, ears turning in all directions like built-in radar.

The shutter clicked. I got him! That's just as good an emotional high as when you complete a difficult shot and have your game down. I want just one more shot, but he stamps his foot, trying to entice more noise or movement from the shape to confirm his suspicion that something threatening to him is there. He looks back at the brush, psossibly thinking of an escape, and takes it in one leap.

He is gone!

Leaning back against the tree, my breathing now back to normal, I'm pleased with the opportunity to get a few photos. That's not always the case, even when I'm shooting in a game refuge or in a park reserve where deer photography is a year-round pursuit. But now its only September, with the best opportunities to come when the leaves drop and the frosty mornings arrive.

This was the third time this week I'd risen early to make the trek to the refuge, to set up my stool and tripod and to get myself comfortable for what may be a long day. Finally I finished a roll of film, but that's the way it is with wildlife photography. Sometimes I shoot two rolls in an hour; at other times it takes two weeks to shoot a single roll.

Today I got restless and walked slowly through the woods, looking for open clearings where I have good light for a photograph, and getting an occasional shot. The really good photos seem always to come while sitting and waiting for deer to move through an area I've staked out. You must have very similar experiences, awaiting the appearance of a good rack or a yearling, even a fat doe.

Try it sometime, but don't forget about light. Enjoy the experience and go back again after that buck, shoot him all over again — with the camera, of course.

JOHN D. LaMERE
Minnetonka, Minnesota

Thirteen-Year-Old Boy's First Hunt

It was my first deer hunt and I had to stay close to Dad even though I was fresh out of gun training. My older brothers went with others in our party.

Dad and I were in the pickup thinking we would drive around the section when a big buck jumped up and ran in the direction from which we had just come. So Dad put the pickup in reverse and we hurriedly backed up.

It was kind of like that song of the woman doing five in reverse, applying mascara in the rear-view mirror, and hollering at the kids. Dad kind of lost control and we went in the ditch, stopping at a sharp angle. Now this was probably a typical farm pickup with the dash full of things like seed corn planning books, electric insulators, tools, a plastic coffee mug, and, of course, shotgun shells. Everything flew past me and out my open window. I reached out and caught the most important things. Just as I was saying that to Dad, I caught the shells; the bottom of the box broke open and the shells landed all over the ground.

Others in the party had watched this little episode and all day long they kept asking if I needed to go home to change my underwear.

DAVID NELSON
Ivanhoe, Minnesota

Many Crazy Things Have Happened

Yes, many crazy things have happened to me while deer hunting, but this story is a little different.

I was bow hunting with nothing going on, so I left my stand to build myself another one. I had brought the material I needed to build one and had left my bow and arrows back at the stand.

When I was hammering boards into the three poplars, a young buck, about a six- or eight-pointer, came out about twenty yards away, not paying any attention to me at all. He just kept eating grass while I kept pounding away. This continued for about twenty minutes, until about fifteen yards north of me a really nice buck of one to twelve points jumped the fence.

I could hardly believe this, and he started to eat and to dig around too, as if he were making a scrape. I watched for a while then went back to pounding nails in the trees, while they acted as if I weren't even there, while my bow was at the other stand. I thought Mother Nature was playing a joke on me. The God's truth.

GARY FRENCH
Sebeka, Minnesota

A Wounded Deer Hunter Struggles for Life

It was early Sunday morning a few years ago when I received a call notifying me that my son, Don, had been shot in the leg while deer hunting and had been taken to the hospital at Park Rapids, Minnesota. At first it didn't sound too serious, but when I telephoned the hospital I learned that he was in critical condition.

When we arrived at the hospital we learned that his heart had stopped several times and that he had no pulse or blood pressure when admitted to the hospital. They had resuscitated him several times and finally, after twenty-five minutes, got a faint heartbeat. He had completely "bled out" following a massive hole in his thigh. We were informed that he was barely alive and very possibly might not make it. Obviously his condition was much worse than "critical." They had worked on him in surgery for four hours, then decided there was nothing more they could do and had transferred him by helicopter to North Memorial Hospital in Minneapolis.

When we arrived at North Memorial in late afternoon we were told that he probably would die before morning, and if he lived, he undoubtedly would be in a vegetative state. He had failed four preliminary tests to determine if there was any brain activity. Of course we were devastated.

Don lay in a coma for nearly six weeks, during which time the specialists could give us no hope because everything in his body had shut down—his kidneys and his lungs had collapsed, and he was being kept alive by what someone called "heroic measures," tubes and machines. Following those many weeks with many ups and downs, with no hope for the future, he started waking up shortly before Christmas. Even today the doctors tell us they don't really know why he is alive.

We know it was truly an answer to the prayers of our many friends; it was an answer from God.

Today he has his good job back in Maple Plain, but he walks with a limp, has a lot of pain, but otherwise leads a normal life. We have much for which we are thankful.

Jim Klobuchar wrote an article about Don which was carried

on the front page of the (Minneapolis) *Star-Tribune* shortly be-fore Christmas, calling it "The Christmas Miracle."

We have kept such detailed records of this period that we have twenty-one typewritten pages of the day-to-day, minute-to-minute events of his recovery.

MARILYN HAMILTON
Maple Plain, Minnesota

Mike

I want to tell you about Mike. Of course, that was a nickname, an abbreviation, because his name was really L. L. Michaels, one of the letters standing for Leo.

For many reasons everyone liked Mike. If you were in an awkward spot it was good to have Mike present, not for safety's sake, but because he was solid, dependable, and always cool headed. As a coach of football and swimming in one of the Iron Range school systems, he'd been around so long producing winning teams and young men of fine mettle that everyone for miles around knew him. He was twenty-five or thirty years older than me when we first got acquainted, one of that small group of men with whom I hunted Up North and sometimes fished in Canada.

Mike knew the territory because he had traveled it so much; in the summer he took groups of high school and college young men into the wilds of Canada on backpack trips to fish those beautiful lakes. I'm sure the young men benefited because Mike wouldn't have made the effort without those goals having been the primary ones.

He knew the woods and how to get along in them. Three years before I met him, he had played a major role in bringing his group of five men out of the woods during the worst blizzard ever to hit Minnesota. (See *All Hell Broke Loose*, by William H. Hull.)

If I were filming the story of Paul Bunyon, I would have wished Mike could play the title role while still in his middle years. He would have been a natural. He seemed bigger than he actually was, but his barrel chest and thickening waist made him appear very large and his booming voice echoed through the woods. When I saw him out in those woods, away from the cabin, wearing multiple layers of jackets and shirts, plus a large pair of Korean winter boots, he seemed nearly gigantic.

Those boots of Mike's surely left their trails; his tracks were quickly identifiable because no other member of our group could leave such an impression. He had probably obtained them from a war surplus store because they were very unusual.

For years the area where we hunted was under contract to a

lumberman who hired other men to cut trees for him during the winter. These men were called gyppoes because they were rumored to gyp the boss in any way possible; actually they probably were hard-working fellows who could stand the loneliness of being in the woods by themselves all winter with little human contact. The boss furnished the crude cabin casually and brought food and supplies on occasion. There were several of these crude shacks in the area we hunted and we always had access to one which was unoccupied.

Bear in mind that the cabins had been built and were unfinished—one-inch crude stock over a bare framework, then covered with one layer of tar paper. The lumber, being unseasoned, had warped while the strong northwinds had usually ripped away a lot of the old tarpaper. So the place was crude. Furnished with four or five built-in bunks, a table, and well-worn, scavenged chairs, a kerosene lamp, and a stove. The stove was the masterpiece. It was made from an iron barrel, laid on its side, fitted into a frame of small I-bars welded together with a door at one end and a flat sheet welded to the top for cooking purposes. A stove pipe led through the roof.

He would awaken us before daybreak.

"Okay, guys. Roll out. We've got to get going. It's getting light in the east and soon we've got to be on our stands."

"Come on! Come on!" he'd roar while banging on a pan, and we'd scramble for our pants and a chance to go outside to the two-holer, but that's another story.

If Mike had a credo about food it was his frequently uttered statement—"You've got to stoke the furnace, boys. Come on, eat up." And he would encourage us to eat more heartily.

Breakfast was a mankiller. Lots of food. Too much food.

Orange juice, unless it was frozen solid. Coffee so strong some of us couldn't handle it. Then he'd direct one of us to make toast on the flat top of the stove and to slather it with butter. In the meantime he was frying bacon by the pound, apparently believing each of us should eat at least a half a pound of it.

Then with the bacon fried he'd start the eggs. They too were to be fried. The problem was that he never removed any of the bacon grease from that big iron skillet and now would start dropping eggs into that scalding fat, saying, "Come on, boys, you've got to stoke the furnace. Eat some more. Each of you needs at least four."

Like cattle being led to slaughter, we'd eat. Exhausted from a lousy night's sleep, maybe fatigued from a hard day's work the previous day in the woods, and perhaps a little too long a swig on the bourbon bottle, we'd eat.

Then we'd finish dressing. At least one pair of underwear, heavy socks, shirt, extra-heavy boots, perhaps insulated, another shirt, jacket(s), heavy headgear with earmuffs, big leather choppers with removeable woolen mitten innerliners, a candy bar or peanuts stuffed in the pockets and, rifle in hand, get out in the brightening day.

Then each man would go through the woods, down the trails, to his own stand, which could be anything from a perch in a tree to sitting quietly atop a tree stump left by the woodcutters.

Nothing deterred our determined approach to our predetermined spot except to vomit or perhaps have an attack of diarrhea from all that fat. That's the reason we carried red toilet paper.

Then we were to hunt all day, not to return to the shack for food at noon because Mike insisted we not eat again until the evening meal. Stoke the furnace well and it won't need any more fuel all day. That may have been okay if we could have managed to keep the food in our bodies all day long, but . . .

The evening meals were better. My Carol, or her sister, Lucille, Andy's wife, would have provided a hot dish or a huge roast, all now frozen and needing the stovetop treatment. Plus exotic things like cookies.

This same group had also made fishing trips into Canada for many years before I came along. They liked to tell of the time when they were up on Koochiching or Elbow, or some other lake I had never heard of before, and an incident that occurred up there.

They were catching fabulous pike (ever notice how the fishing was always superb on the trips you didn't get to take?) and Mike was preparing breakfast around an outdoor campfire.

As he fried the bacon, this time he poured off the grease into a handy empty beer bottle, left over from the previous night. One of the guys saw it, thought it was a leftover bottle of night-cooled beer and took a healthy swig.

"Hell's bells!" he yelled, sputtering to get the warm oil from his mouth, "What in the hell is that?" You can believe that someone told him, with great humor.

For some reason that reminds me of an occurrence in a Twin Cities hospital emergency room which, by occurrence, I just happened to observe.

Three men in their early thirties brought in a comrade who had severe facial burns. What happened? They were camping Up North and that morning during a scuffle one fell face first into the open campfire, getting badly burned. The group had driven about three hundred miles with that poor fellow before getting him medical attention. They had bypassed three or four towns in which hospitals could have provided the care that patient needed. Ladies, watch your men. Sometimes we can be really stupid under the guise of being macho.

Dear ol' Mike's time finally came. First he lost Ruth, his wife of many years, then lived alone in their lovely home, keeping contacts with his many fishing and hunting buddies and getting his share of young deer and big lunkers. At somewhere in his nineties (someone said one hundred, but I don't believe that) he passed away.

He was a good man, a man who lived life gloriously, helped a lot of boys into manhood, knew some outstanding men, like Bronko Nagurski, one of the greatest football playes of all time, who lived not too far away Up North in International Falls.

Yes. A good man. And a good friend.

BILL HULL

Grandfather Teaches Grandson the Old Way

(An interview)

You've done some deer hunting, too, Bob, not just bull moose hunting. What's the most interesting experience you ever had when after deer?

One of the best, but it didn't amount to much, was with my grandson who's in the middle in that picture. He's my deer hunting partner. My other two grandsons weren't interested in hunting.

Yes, everyone doesn't get the bug.

Anyway, I had to do chores in the morning, so we didn't get an early start. I don't know whether you know where Markville, Cloverton, and Kingsdale are, but they're near the Wisconsin-Minnesota border.

Sure, sure.

Back in the sixties we did a lot of hunting near Kingsdale. One trip, it was about 10:30 in the morning when we got there, I looked across the road and said to Brian, "Look at that deer cross the road. It's a buck and it's wounded. I know by the way it runs." Neither one of us got off a shot. So we checked the trail and found some spots of blood. So we stopped and had a sandwich, the hunter's time to catch up, you know.

We waited there for quite a time, but no one showed up.

Nobody was trailing it?

Right. I said we'd better go. But we hadn't gone very far when we saw it and I said, "There he goes, Brian. Better shoot it. He hadn't shot a deer that big. He said, "I can't see it." So I got in a shot, but of course I missed it. He left a pretty good blood trail . . . and then the chase was on. There was no snow, but I'd done a lot of tracking. We were real careful and found blood on both sides of the trail. Sometimes high, sometimes low. I told Brian I couldn't understand the difference in the height of the blood marks. But we kept trailing until about 3:00 in the afternoon I told Brian that I was bushed and had to sit down and have a bite to eat. It was in the fall and getting dark already and I thought we had lost the trail. We sat awhile and ate. I soon got a little more energy, so I told Brian I'm going to make one last circle while you wait here.

I found a grassy swamp with water and I said to myself that he went through that trail. So I went through that water and, lo and behold, there he laid in the brush. So I whistled to Brian to come on over and finish it. He was shot in the jaw. That explained why there had been bloodstains both high and low on the trail.

Brian was fifteen and I was sixty, starting to go downhill, and we realized we'd have to find a way to get that deer out of there. We knew we'd have to compass to get out of there, as we pulled him with a rope. We'd line up a tree ahead and head for it with the compass. I knew the road ahead ran north and south and, being the older one of the two of us, had to step forward. We went through water this deep—you can't go around a swamp, particularly in the dark.

Soon we saw a yard light. I told Brian to take the two rifles and go ahead to the house while I'd continue to drag out the deer. But, I told him, if you get out to the pickup and a hunter is waiting, it's his deer. That's the old code. Tell them they can have the deer— it's theirs rightfully— we had the pleasure of hunting it and getting it down. Of course we were willing to forget all the work of dragging it out through the swamp.

True enough, when he got to the car, hunters were there and Brian told them what I had suggested. "No," said the hunter. "It's your deer. You brought it in through that swamp. The only thing we want is that the guy who shot it wants to know where he hit it."

That settled it.

Brian came out within a hundred feet of our pickup and started it until we got warm. They insisted we go to their camp saying, "It's good that you got him. We didn't want it to go to waste."

Now I'm the old way. Whoever first draws blood, it's his deer. Today some fellows won't let it be that simple, but the old way was better.

Yes, you're an honest man, Bob.

Well, Brian learned a good lesson that day, and I'm glad it happened that way.

I remember one of my early hunting trips, Bob, when I shot a deer but couldn't catch up with it in the woods. I figured I'd lost it. As we were packing out late that afternoon here was a "gyppo"* standing on the trail with a dead deer, which he wanted to sell me for $20. I told him, Bob, that it was my deer, but he insisted that he had shot it, so I just turned and went on down the trail. I knew exactly where my rifle lead had hit it and that was exactly where this deer was hit. My claiming it meant nothing to this guy; he just wanted the money so, as Mike said, "He could just skip out cross country for the nearest settlement with money for booze and a woman."

ROBERT LOFGREN
Rush City, Minnesota

* A gyppo in Up North slang is a woodcutter who works in the woods during the winter, living in a shack supplied with food by the landowner and/or land leaser, and was paid by the cord of wood he cut. I suspected some early boss thought the woodcutter cheated him in some way in the winter and thus the word "gyppo" was coined, as unfair as it probably was.

On Crutches, Hunting from a Lawn Chair

While bowling a few years ago I felt something snap suddenly in my left knee. There wasn't any pain so I continued with my game.

But the next morning, when we were leaving for a trip to the cabin, I could feel a snap in that knee at every step. So I went for medical help. The doctor said the cartilages in that knee had all come loose, and I was immediately scheduled for surgery. After the surgery came time with the leg in an elastic cast up to the hip, and then came crutches.

Since I had already purchased my deer license that year, I thought I might as well go through with it, to the extent possible. With my wife and son we took off for the cabin to hunt. The cabin is located on the river in Park Rapids.

On opening day my son went back into the woods and got his deer. The wife carried a lawn chair to a spot where I could watch both the woods and the river. I followed along on crutches and spent the day uneventfully.

At four o'clock I went back out for the final hour. I was busy watching a great horned owl and a pileated woodpecker when I heard a sound across the river. I thought it was hunters so didn't pay much attention until I heard it again. I looked over my shoulder, and lo and behold, a buck was drinking directly across the river. Just as I shot, he jumped. Damned it! I missed.

He didn't jump far. All I could see was a spot of his shoulder between a vee of a birch tree, so I shot again. Bull's-eye this time. Meantime the wife had decided to see what was going on. She opened the sliding door of the cabin facing the river and, in her excitement, came barreling out, forgetting to open the screen door. All I saw was a screen followed by my wife.

My son came out of the woods. He and my wife went to get the boat so the son could retrieve the deer. The wife came back to pick up the canoe paddles and we watched our son paddling across the river, breaking ice. While watching, I looked down to see a big fat raccoon which was ambling almost across my feet. I could have hit it with my crutch; he had been sleeping in the boat and my son had kicked him out when he got in to cross the river. The son decided he didn't want to argue with a grumpy old raccoon.

The deer? Sure, it was a nice five-point buck.

IRWIN SWANSON
Richfield, Minnesota

Ten Degrees on the Floor,
One Hundred in the Upper Bunk . . .

. . . wind howling against the shack's walls, cold air blowing through the cracks.

Living, if you can call it that, in a deer shack, can be about anything from staying in a crude woodchopper's shack to a deserted wooden building last used a few years ago and left standing because it was too dangerous to burn it to the ground. It's a long, long way from a modern motel accommodation. And it's apt to be a long way back in the woods.

Ours was just that, several miles off the main road, down a rutted neglected logging trail not used for years except for an occasional load of deer hunters searching for an abandoned shack. For many years, our shack was provided free by a friend of Andy's, who had built a few of these one-inch board buildings as shelters for his winter woodcutters, whom everyone called gyppos because it was said they gypped the boss out of a good day's work. The deal was that they lived in the shack and worked days in the extreme cold, felling trees and cutting them into proper lengths to be trucked to the sawmill where they usually were made into chips for chipboard or pressed wood, or even toothpicks or chopsticks. (It was a joke of the region that Minnesotans made chopsticks to sell to the Chinese because we could make them more cheaply.) The boss's obligation was to show up at the shack with food and other supplies. If he didn't show up, Andy's friend said, his gyppo would just walk away, go to town, find a bottle and a woman, maybe go back to the job, maybe not. So the boss had to be regular or he had no woodcutter.

Anyway, this friend of Andy's had an unused gyppo shack to which he directed us for several years. I could find my way to it, but can't describe it except that we left the highway north of Cook, Minnesota, to drive to the end of the world, or so it seemed. Frequently it meant moving a windblown tree from the road so we could move ahead.

We pulled off the road, put on all of the clothing possible, picked up a knapsack full of heavy stuff, our sleeping bag, a rifle, heavy chopper gloves. Of course we were also wearing heavy boots and very warm hats. Then off we went down the trail, skirting the beaver dam, and into the woods. It wasn't too far to the shack, just about all-you-could-possibly-move-before-dropping dead distance. Then, there in a small clearing, sat our Shangri-La. Dark, foreboding, deathly, no sign of light or life, unless one of our group had arrived early, started a fire and lighted a coal-oil lamp or lantern. It was to be our home for about three nights.

Urp!

Really, though, it had all the comforts of home. (Not my home!)

There was running water; you had to run out in the subzero temperature through the snow about fifty feet, chop a hole in the ice, grab a bucketful of true ice water, run back to the house with it, and hug the fire to thaw.

There was hot water also, providing you could put a pan or two atop the stove, build a fire in the stove, and wait for it to warm. There was also hot coffee, hot chocolate, or hot cereal.

It had a hastily built outdoor toilet (Chic Sale, to some of you), a place again to which you ran scantily dressed, performed your duties, then ran back to huddle against the stove or perhaps return to bed.

Our shack had been built of crude one-inch boards from a nearby lumberyard, covered with tar paper and strips of wood (lathes) covering the seams of the basic framework and holding down the tar paper. Of course, that tar paper was a constant challenge for the strong northern Minnesota winds, which usually found a vulnerable corner and tore away some of the tar paper. The reader will understand why, when the outside temperature was below zero, and the windchill was down to the ground, we sometimes talked about our air-conditioned quarters.

The central piece of furniture was the stove, which was an iron barrel standing on a base of angle iron welded into a frame to keep it off the floor. A hole had been cut in one end and an iron-hinged door attached. At the other end, atop the stove, was another hole, with a cuff welded atop, to which chimney pipe could be attached and sent up through the roof. Atop the barrel, now on its side, had been welded a large piece of flat iron to create a stove top, a flat area for cooking.

That stove could get hot. In fact, it usually was red-hot before we got it under control, but it took a lot of wood to do that. The cook could place several pans or skillets atop that stove (remember, it is laying on its side) as well as toast bread directly on that flat top. And heat! With that thing red hot, that small garage-sized shack was usually so warm we sat around with heavy jacket, heavy shirt, removed, but not the boots. That floor never got up much above zero.

As a wood-burning monster, we had to provide the firewood. Sometimes the previous occupant(s) had left some cut cordwood outside, but usually, we had to cut or scrounge enough to keep the fire going for three days. Nights, too, because if you let that fire go completely out, there was hell to pay trying to keep alive in a sleeping bag, augmented with a wool blanket, your heavy underwear, and perhaps extra socks.

You've never encountered real cold until you experienced that situation.

No, we did not have to sleep on the floor, because someone in the distant past had built bunks, two high. There were usually just enough bunks for our group of four to six, but the difference in temperature in the different height bunks was considerable. The fellows in the lower level remained cold all night while the upper level occupants sweat, sometimes profusely.

And let me assure you, when a man has sweat in his bunk for three nights, as well as sweating when dragging a deer back to the camp, usually in the same clothing, he becomes notable. Or is it notable or noteworthy? In any case, when you start home in a crowded automobile, the conglomerate becomes a diSTINKtive mob.

Elsewhere in this book, I've already told of Mike's preparation of breakfasts over that stove—he did a masterful and memorable job.

So, the shack was a very important place for us. It was home, if you can call it that, but not home as anyone ever described home before. It did give us shelter and a headquarters. When you have spent all day long in the woods, walking constantly or sitting on a cold stand, perhaps up in a windswept tree, you're happy to return to camp to share the day's experiences with friends, to have a cup of hot coffee or maybe a couple of slugs of brandy. Then too much heavy food, a little talk, climbing into the sack to keep warm, and trying to get to sleep before the other guys start snoring like buzzsaws—yet they all insist that they don't snore. "You're crazy. I never snore." "Then," someone always asks, "why in hell does Matilda make you sleep in another room?"

Then finally comes the last day, when you have to haul everything out through the woods, down the rough lumbering trail, across the beaver dam, and out to the cars. Not to forget the deer carcasses, of which there are usually one for each man. As Mike would say, "Strip down to your bare top. That way you won't catch a cold. You'll sweat, sure, but when you get to the car, start putting the layers back on, one at a time. Just as you get cool with that layer then add another." He was correct, too. As you get hot, peel off a layer at a time to reach a comfort zone. In reverse, as you are through exercising or working and start to get cold, add a layer at a time, keeping dry and just cool. That way you avoid problems.

But it's a great world. I just wish I could do it again. As my friend, Rob Lofgren, said the other day: "I told my doctor the other day that I'm going moose hunting in Canada again this fall although I've had all this heart surgery and am over seventy-six years old." I wasn't told the physician's reply.

WILLIAM H. HULL
Edina, Minnesota

My Deer Turned Out to be a Gigantic Bull Moose

Yes, that's true, but I wasn't hunting deer. I was on a once-in-a-lifetime trip hunting moose up in northern British Columbia and hoping I'd be lucky enough to get a Boone & Crockett–sized animal. But before I tip off the story, let me tell you about it in sequence.

With a friend and hunting companion, Jon Alvin, I had flown in to the airport at Fort Nelson, British Columbia, (the northeast corner of British Columbia) where we were met by our guide, a tall, raw-boned man named Ted Cobbett, who would turn out to be a good friend by the time this trip was over. We were looking forward with mixed emotions to a seven-mile drive to the ranch, from whence we would be flown to our ultimate destination, Cobbett's spike camp near the Liard River valley, close to the Yukon border. A "spike camp," in case the term is unfamiliar to you, is an outpost camp, of which Cobbett had several in the territory he covered, which was a piece of land 8,400 square miles in size.

It was October and chilly when we arrived at the ranch, with six feet of snow on the ground, a big change from what I had left in Minnesota where, just five days previously, I had watched my son's high-school football game comfortably in a sweater.

We soon had stashed our gear in a guest cabin, joined Cobbett's family for dinner, and settled in for a night of dreaming about trophy moose.

What is a trophy moose? Let me put it this way. On the plane from Minneapolis to Edmonton, Alberta, I had read about an Alaskan hunter who had confronted a seventy-two-inch bull moose as he rounded a corner trail on a horse. What an enormous animal that must have been! And what a shock both hunter, horse, and moose must have had!

The early start the next day saw us raring to go. Cobbett had decided that Alvin would be the first to fly in with him in the Super Cub two-seater to the spike camp, while I spent time sorting out my gear. It wasn't long before it was my time to be packed aboard, with my cased Ruger 7mm Magnum and duffel bag. Cobbet threw in a guitar case, and I was glad to see that we'd have some nighttime music around the fire, inside or outside, whichever it might be.

Forty-five minutes later we were at the spike camp, which needs description. Two eight-by-eight-foot log cabins with a slightly larger cook shack and storehouse constituted the camp. Our first job, however, was to round up the horses and induce them into the corral with a bucketful of oats, so we could latch the corral gates behind them. I hadn't realized how they would provide horses in the midst of this large area. They had been ridden in earlier in the season and left there with food and water, in between organized hunts. I believe there was a guide who checked on them regularly. There wasn't much natural food for them in this remote area, so they relied heavily on the oats-from-home basic food. The season was tough on them, and by the end of the season, they had lost weight and were ready for greener pastures and rest back at the main ranch.

After dinner it was fun to hear Cobbett reminisce about his years as an outfitter and guide, particularly a recent experience of one of his hunters who nailed the current Boone & Crockett Club world record Canada moose back in 1980. His outfit, the Scatter River Outfitters, had exclusive hunting rights in an area approximately 120 miles long and 70 miles wide.

The next morning at first light, we were ready to saddle up and load our gear for the day's ride. Since neither Alvin nor I had done a lot of riding recently, I for one (I don't really know about Alvin) was not really ready for the long, rugged trip the day would probably show, as we went into the wilderness.

While we were down in the valley, the snow was only about three inches deep, but soon we were in waist-deep snow in the upper mountains. I'll long remember the treat of drinking fresh, very cold water right from the creeks.

We rode steadily until 3 P.M., moving around bogs, through creeks, up hillsides, and through ten-foot-high brush, finally stopping just below the crest of a small mountain, where we secured the horses.

Climbing cautiously on foot we reached the crest of the ridge, peeked carefully over the opposite side of the basin where Cobbett said he'd seen a lot of sign in the area, particularly that of some big bulls. Thinking we were in danger of alarming our quarry with our scent, we were about to backtrack when Cobbett said, "There—over there in that opening." As we glassed the area where he was pointing, we could see the antler palms of a large bull which was standing and looking directly at us. He was nervous and about ready to retreat, although he already looked to be about 350 yards away. Since we had already agreed that Alvin would take the the first moose, I stepped back, ready to watch the action. "You'd better take your shot Buds," Cobbett warned, "cuz he's moving off." Alvin took a quick rest and touched off three shots from his 30-06. I heard a couple of the shots hit, when Cobbett motioned for me to shoot. As the bull was about to move off, I was able to fire twice before he disappeared. Cobbett confirmed that the bull was hit and said he had seen the animal go down.

At about the same time, farther back in the basin, we saw another bull linger and then move into a thicket before I could shoot. That second bull was also big, definitely trophy material.

Cobbett supervised our mounting up to get over to the fallen moose, which we found dead where Cobbett had seen him go down. Alvin's bull was a real trophy, and Cobbett said the antlers should make the Boone & Crockett record book. Then we could see that Alvin had hit the bull with two shots and that only one of mine had connected. Immediately I thought of the possibility that my sights better be rechecked at the first opportunity. I'd do that when we returned to the camp.

We butchered the animal, enjoyed a Spam* sandwich and a cup of hot field-made coffee and loaded the meat, the rack, and the cape onto the horses for the ride back to the camp. Needless to say, Alvin's spirits were at an all-time high, deservedly, too, I must add.

I don't believe I've ever seen a more welcome sight than the light that was on in the cook shack when we finally reached the camp late that night. An Indian guide, known to us only as Roy A., had arrived and greeted us warmly. After dinner, Cobbett pulled out his guitar and serenaded us with some twangy country western music, which made me admire him even more, for his abilities and his carefree attitude in the wild. He surely knew his business.

I judged Cobbett to be in his mid-thirties, six-feet-two-inches tall, and about 180 pounds. He looked lean and hard, a fit man. He's an accomplished bush pilot, hunter, guide, outfitter, woodsman, and guitarist. I got the feeling that he could be dropped anywhere in the world and he'd be entirely self-sufficient. He also seemed to have a sixth sense about where game would move daily, which was one of the qualities I liked best.

We went to sleep feeling good. There was already one big bull in camp and I was hoping I'd have a chance to get a big one, too, at least as large, or maybe even bigger.

When I resighted my rifle the next day I found my suspicion to be right. The scope had been jarred just enough to be off.

We split up for the day. Alvin had obtained permits also for both black bear and grizzly bear and he and Cobbett went off in pursuit of a nine and a half-foot grizzly that had been seen in the area the week before we arrived. Roy A. and I made up the other team and we headed for Moose Mountain, a favorite spot for big bulls to rest after the rutting season.

We proceeded up a long ridge, through some brush, some woods, and then across several creeks. When we neared a flat saddle in between two mountains, Roy stopped and looked at a nearby tree. On a branch in that tree clung a defiant marten, angry at us for invading his territory and cussing at us. Roy looked at him longingly, I thought, and remarked, "His fur is worth $190," shaking his head, probably thinking that had I not been along he could have taken the animal and been $190 richer.

As we were moving on up the side of the mountain, I noticed the horses were cocking their ears and looking into some timber at the right of us. I suspected it was some sort of an animal, but I couldn't see anything. In a few minutes we stopped to let the horses rest briefly and, lo and behold, out walked a nice-sized-bull moose down below us. He followed our tracks for about fifty yards before beginning to eat his way through the brush on the saddle which we had just crossed. Roy wanted me to go back to stalk the bull but I demurred, saying I wanted a trophy bull or no bull at all. Again he shook his head.

After taking a slightly different trail back to the camp, it was long after dark when we saw the cabin lights; Cobbett and Alvin had blanked that day, too, but we were all in good spirits; it wasn't long after dinner when I fell into bed for the night, only to be greeted the next morning by Cobbett's question, "You up to a hard ride today?" to which I replied, "Sure." "See that range of mountain overpointing a long snowy ridge in the distance?" I swallowed hard, knowing it wouldn't be easy to get there. "Let's go, Buds."

I never did know specifically what he meant by that word "Buds."

He wasn't kidding about the hard ride. We crossed hills, creeks, and half-frozen bogs before beginning to work our way up into the range of mountains. At about one o'clock we stopped at another one of Cobbett's spike camps, which sometimes were nothing more than a couple of boards nailed to a tree to mark spots where he's left supplies.

Over a cup of thermos coffee, Cobbett said, "We're going up on the tundra where it'll be windy and cold, so button up cuz it'll be rough when we get there." I must say, however, that no one was better prepared for a moose hunter than I was. In Edmonton I even showered with Scent Shield and Body Soap, a product that eliminates human odor. I knew it might be my last chance for a shower during the days ahead.

Again he spoke the truth as up in the high tundra we encountered blinding snow and quartering winds that approached sixty miles per hour. We moved along the frigid ridge for a couple of hours before he stopped to rest the horses.

During our rest, conditions became worse. I could make out only a faint gray outline of Cobbett and his mount ahead of me, and the left side of my face felt like it was beginning to freeze. I placed my cupped hand over my cheek every hundred feet or so to keep it warm.

After what seemed like an eternity, Cobbett moved us off the crest of the mountain to the side of a valley. We secured the horses to some rocks and Cobbett motioned for me to grab my gun and follow. We scrambled down the valley side until we reached the tree line, then I started glassing the valley below. The snow was still blowing and it was somewhat more comfortable. At 3 p.m. I figured it was another bust day.

Suddenly Cobbett gave that signal of the right thumb jerking upward, which I had grown to know meant "Game sighted!" I panned along his line of sight and caught a pair of giant antler palms against the snow. It was huge and he appeared to be looking directly at us. Could he see that far? Cobbett motioned me to follow him as he crept down the valley side of the mountain, through the trees. There was a crosswind between the bull and us, which meant there was a chance he would catch our scent. At 450 yards, Cobbett stopped and said, "Can you get him from here, Buds?"

"You've got to be kidding," I replied. "I don't have confidence in this shot." The bull was in a small thicket and still at a steep angle from us on the opposite side of the valley. I wanted to get closer so I'd have a more level shot, while Cobbett was concerned about the moose bolting.

Later I was pleased I had used that new product called Scent Shield, which is so potent it completely wipes out human scent and an animal cannot smell the hunter. Not at all. Best such product I have ever used.

We moved farther down the valley and again the guide paused.

"You're going to have to take your shot from here. He won't wait."

I found a fallen tree and rested my rifle across it for support.

"Where should I hold?" I asked.

"High on the shoulder. When you come down with the scope, you'll have plenty of time to squeeze off your shots."

I lined up the crosshairs of the Leupold 3 to 9 scope on the top of the bull's back, then took a deep breath and released it slowly. I estimated that it was 350 yards to the target. I slowly squeezed off my first round—my best shot, I thought—but nothing happened.

The moose stood rigid. Still.

I fired again, but the bull still didn't stir. One more shot. Nothing. I turned to Cobbett in disbelief.

"What happened?"

"You hit him twice," he whispered, as the bull walked slowly behind a clump of pines. "You missed the first shot, but you hit him with the next two."

I nervously fumbled for more shells; I wanted to catch the bull when he came out the other side of the pines, but nothing happened.

Cobbett pondered the situation for a few minutes.

"I think he's down, but I can't be sure," the guide said. "One of us has to go up after the horses and the other has to go after the bull."

"Guess who's going after the horses?" I laughed nervously.

"Here. Take my 30-30," he whispere, "cuz that scoped gun of yours won't do you a bit of good at close range. He's somewhere close to that stand of pines, so use that as a reference point and make a circle downwind so he can't smell you."

We parted company, and I started for the valley floor, sneaking as quietly as possible. When I got down there I was amazed to find that the brush was ten feet high and no way could I see the stand of pines. Moving cautiously in a large semicircle around where I thought the pines were, I couldn't help thinking of a giant wounded bull charging me. I made doubly sure there was a shell chambered in Cobbett's rifle.

Since I hadn't cut any fresh tracks by the time I reached the far side of the valley, I knew that the bull was still in the area, but where? I slowly worked my way to where I thought I'd last seen the monster.

I then spotted the unmistakable form of the huge fallen bull.

I approached the fallen animal slowly, and when a prod in the haunches produced no reaction, I moved forward. That was the moment I realized how truly huge the moose was, spending the next few moments admiring the magnificent animal. What a great feeling to know that he was mine!

I pulled off my red vest and tied it high in a pine tree so that Cobbett could spot me in the blowing snow. I then started skinning the moose.

Soon the guide rode up, tied the horses to some trees, then came over and looked down at the moose. "You know what you've got there, Buds?" he asked, after a brief silence.

"Yeah, I've got myself a big bull," I grinned.

"You've got yourself a world record," he announced. "You just shot the King of the Mountain."

My first thought was that Cobbett was simply trying to make me feel good. I didn't think it was possible for a guy to simply look at a moose in the field and make an accurate judgment about something like that. But the guide was grinning from ear to ear and that wasn't quite like him.

It was hard work skinning the bull. The hide was so tough that I had to stop and put a new edge on my knife every few minutes. I looked up and noticed that the weather had gotten worse again, and we both began working furiously to get the job done.

We packed the rack, the cape, and the meat on the horses and began the climb back to the high tundra. Visibility was terrible and Cobbett estimated that the temperature had dropped to ten degrees below zero.

Yes, going was rough. It took us about three hours to get back to the small spike camp where we had made coffee earlier, and we still had a long distance left to the cabins.

At 1 A.M. we finally rode into camp, but despite the time, Alvin and Roy were up like a flash to greet us. We rehashed the story for their benefit. I grabbed a cup of soup and collapsed into my bed.

The next morning Cobbett was holding forth in the cook shack, pulling out his Boone & Crockett book. He had already measured the bull's rack three times.

"Yes, it's a world's record all right," he said. "The bull has a 63½-inch spread and 'green scored' 244 points"—exceeding the score of the 1980 record bull taken by Cobbett's client by two points. Only then did the idea start sinking in for me. Cobbett was so excited that he suggested we tie the rack to his plane and fly to the ranch, then go directly to Fort Nelson.

Alvin and Roy decided to keep trying for bear while they brought the stock out of the mountains for the winter, so it was agreed they would hunt their way out with the horse string.

We closed up the camp, flew to the ranch for a short stop, then on to Fort Nelson, where our reception was something I'll never forget. Although Cobbett suggested I stay another day to extend the party, I was so worn-out and tired I felt I'd better head for home.

Besides, I'd already gotten what I'd come for. The King of the Mountain would be flying home with me.

The bull was officially recognized as the biggest moose bull ever taken in Canada, and at this writing Boone & Crockett officials have not made the final ruling. It's a very involved procedure, with the rack requiring drying time of ninety days, and official inspection and ruling by an assigned group of Boone & Crockett Club judges, but it looks as if it is final. Apparently, I have the world's record bull moose.

Ernie Peacock
Prior Lake, Minnesota

An Injured Deer by the Roadside

Just before Christmas 1944 I took my wife, my daughter, and my grandson for a ride to west Bloomington to see the homes decorated for the season.

We were driving along a dark road near Bush Lake when I spotted a deer lying in the ditch at the right side of the road. It appeared to have been hit by a car or a snowplow and was nearly buried in the deep snow.

We continued on to see the lights, visiting most of the neighborhoods in that area, then after forty to forty-five minutes, we headed home. Ryan, my thirteen-year-old grandson, asked if I could find the deer again. I soon found it and we walked across the road to get a closer look.

It was buried in the hard snow except for one rear leg and the side of the stomach. I couldn't see any blood, so I softly pushed on the side of the stomach with my foot, when suddenly the exposed leg moved. I continued to touch it gently with my foot when it suddenly, to our surprise, pulled its head out of that hard snow. It looked at us in a dazed condition then stood up. It walked away about four feet from us, stood there looking at us, watching. Although it was dark, my wife and daughter saw all of this from the car while the deer stood there motionless just watching us, obviously not afraid of us. We assumed all was well with the deer because the next day when we returned to check on it, it was gone.

KENT W. GROBEL
Bloomington, Minnesota

How Do You Transport a Thousand-Pound Dead Moose?

Although I've hunted deer for many years, I also got involved in moose hunting so much that I was given the nickname of "The Old Moose Hunter."

It was during the very first days of October, 1990 when I started to load my pickup and small trailer house to make my thirty-sixth moose hunting trip into Ontario, Canada. When I had completed thirty-five seasons of hunting moose, the year before, I had put my memories into a small book and had it published.*

(Editor: To get to his favorite moose hunting territory, Robert goes into Ontario via Pigeon River in northeast Minnesota, then up Highway 11 to Thunder Bay, Nipigon, Beardmore, and apparently hunts between Jellicoe and Longlac, approximaely 260 kilometers into Canada. A photo accompanies this article showing Rob's huge bull moose taken on October 10, 1990, on his thirty-sixth moose hunting trip, when Rob was seventy.)

I arrived at Wild Goose resort where I had made arrangements for my moose hunt. I hunted north of Jellicoe off the King Horn road for two days without success, so I decided on Wednesday I would drive over to Longlac and hunt with two Indian friends I had known for a long time. Albert Ruben was unable to go with me, so George Ruben and I went. He said he knew a river he wanted to try so we took his boat and motor and drove to the river.

We loaded everything we would need and started down the river. We had gone only a short distance when I felt a little chilly, so I started to button up my coat when I spied a movement on the river bank to our left. At that moment a beautiful bull moose jumped into the water.

It was some distance away so George headed the canoe to the opposite shore. We hit the bank and George shut off the motor. The moose was in shallow water at the edge of the river. As we watched for a moment or two he picked up a windfall with his antlers and threw it into the air, then shook off the water from

his heavy coat of hair. I'll never forget how those drops glistened in the sun.

I thought it was now or never, so I aimed my Winchester .348 at his chest and fired. He never knew what hit him, the bullet hitting him in the neck bone. So, he fell and never moved. Then George said to me, "Robert, last night I got down on my knees and prayed for a moose for you." I thanked him sincerely and he could see how very happy I was.

Then George said to me, "But how do we get him out of here?" (Editor Bill Hull says, "That is exactly what I asked Robert when I first saw the photo of this immense moose. I had asked, how do you handle a thousand pounds of dead moose when there's only two of you back in the outcountry alone? That's a lot of dead weight to move.")

"So," Robert continued, "I told him I didn't think it would be too hard."

I stepped out into the water from the canoe and managed to roll and twist the dead moose into deeper water, where I was, with water up to my waist. George brought the canoe around and I tied a rope to the moose's antlers and to the canoe, then climbed back into the canoe. George gave it some gas, but the moose carcass wouldn't move until he hit it three times to sort of jerk the body to follow the canoe.

When we got to the place where we had put the canoe in the water we managed to roll the moose out with a come along, got it up on the bank; at that point there was a very high, steep bank, leading up to the road.

Just then a gravel truck came by and the driver stopped to ask if we needed help. I told him I had a pickup nearby. He was concerned because he said there were many trucks hauling gravel on that road and, although each truck had a CB in the cab, it was dangerous for us and the moose to be on the roadbed. Then he put a rope on the moose and pulled it to the pickup.

I had started to dress out the moose when another man stopped with his pickup to look at my prize animal. He mentioned that he had a loader close by in the brush and he'd use it to help load the body. Before I could finish dressing out the carcass, here he came with the front-end loader, scooped up that thousand pounds of dead meat, and did the job easily. We were very grateful.

No one could ever have planned a trip like that. In a short time it was talked about everywhere. It was not only the largest moose I ever shot but also the second largest any of my group had ever taken. Of course, I will remember that hunt forever.

I'd had one heart surgery by then so had to be careful; since then I've had another one, which was almost fatal, plus other heart problems. But I was determined to make my fortieth moose trip last fall, October 1995. I had a very nice trip alone, even though I did not get a glimpse of a moose.

I had wanted to hunt moose since I was a young boy, but I was told at age twenty that I couldn't do that because the moose season was closed almost everywhere. Finally conditions changed and I was able to go to Canada to hunt this mammoth animal.

I am now seventy-six years old with forty seasons behind me and feel very fortunate.

The Old Moose Hunter

ROBERT LOFGREN
Rush City, Minnesota

* *35 Seasons of Hunting Memories from the Old Moose Hunter.* Robert Lofgren is a friend of recent years. Although he has been a farmer, a cattle trucker and father to several stalwart sons, he is also known as "The Old Moose Hunter," which I suspect is a self-designated nickname or perhaps he was dubbed that by admirers who know of his thirty-five to forty years of hunting moose predominantly in Canada, also as a highly respected deer hunter. Rob had a boyhood desire to go to Canada to hunt the giant bull moose; he eventually got to pursue it with consistent success. When one sees the photos of his immense trophies one's first question is apt to be, as was mine, "How could you and others handle a thousand pounds of dressed-out dead meat, at a kill site way back in the woods?" One quickly realizes it requires several very strong men or machinery. When telling people about Rob at the 1996 Whitetail Show of the Minnesota Deerhunters Association, people off-handedly said, "You'd have to quarter it and haul it out." Sure, but how many men could carry out a quarter of a thousand pounds? In one instance, a roadworker helped Rob and his Indian friend by returning with a front-end loader to pick up the bull and place it in the pickup's bed.

Be Prepared if You Hunt in Minnesota

It was that time of the year again—deer hunting time.

After a long, slow drive on icy snowpacked roads, we arrived at our destination in the Minnesota northwoods, just before midmorning. In order to get our vehicles into our camp, we had to walk the last half-mile first, shaking heavy snows from the branches of small trees which bent forming arches over the road.

The Old Hunter who each year arrives at camp a few days before the season and who stays a full three weeks each season was quick to tell us that it had rained all day Thursday and snow had developed during the night, dumping six inches of heavy stuff on the ground with at least three inches sticking on the northeast sides of the trees. Smaller trees and brush had collapsed from the weight of the wet sticky snow.

We have a somewhat unusual deer camp. We park two campers about twelve feet apart and put up a canvas tarp between them. We put a pole in the middle of the tarp and raise it up about eight feet; we hang another tarp on the north end for a windbreak.

We put a table under the tarp and do almost all of our cooking on a grill we have brought along. We made a portable outhouse of a wooden box with a real toilet seat on it. We put plastic tarps over and around it. We have a small heater in it. The first hunter to use it in the morning has to light it. This can cause some suffering because no one wants to be that first person to use the cold toilet.

This year we are going to take a portable shower to camp. Same setup as the outhouse but with a wooden pallet for a base. One of my friends is in the camper repair business and will bring a portable generator to camp. We will heat the water over the fire, then put it in a five-gallon bucket. Then with a water pump from an old camper, we will pump water into the shower. What we have done in the past on a midweek morning is to hunt until noon, then grab our clean clothing and drive twelve miles to a bar, have pizza, and take a shower in their basement. It costs us a whole dollar for the shower, but it's worth a million.

Four guys hunt on my cousin's ten-acre wood lot, to the south and the east of the camp road. Three of us from our party hunt state land to the west of our camp.

On Saturday morning, opening day, the trek to my stand, which normally would take thirty minutes, took an hour and thirty minutes. That stand is the last one into the woods and only a half mile from the road. That morning the trip was at least a mile due to the loss of our trail marks. Although we had marked them only a week ago, the trail now was 'gone with the snow.' An occasional ribbon was still in place. Because of that situation we got turned around a few times; landmarks were not there for guidance. Visibility was so limited that the heavy pine stands looked like ridges due to piling of the snow.

That Saturday morning was one of the quietest I have ever experienced on opening morning. Typically, shots are heard for several hours afer legal shooting begins. This morning I counted the gunshots without using the toes on my left foot.

About noontime our party of seven gathered at camp for lunch and a discussion of the morning hunt. Only one deer, a fawn, had been seen by a party member who was in a stand east of the road.

At about 1:30 my partners and I began to amble back to the woods in search of bucks. A vehicle with Illinois plates was parked off the road into the swamp near the spot where we enter the woods. It was from Chicago. The driver was watching the swamp and a small clearing from the comfort of the car, while his friend hunted in the woods no more than fifty yards away; he was unfamiliar with the area.

We continued down the road and entered the woods on the trail leading west. On the way to our own stands we'd encountered the friend of the Chicago hunter. He was perched in the stand nearest the road, at which time he had seen a large doe.

The afternoon hunt was just as productive as the morning's had been. Nothing!

Legal shooting ended on opening day at 4:30. Knowing I had a long trek back to the shack, I decided to get going. En route I soon connected with my buddies and the Chicago man who had been in a tree stand. Soon we saw again the driver of the Chicago vehicle, and we told him his buddy had seen a doe but didn't shoot at it.

We got back to the camp at about 5 P.M. Three of our guys from the east were not in yet. At nearly 5:30, when it was totally dark, a shot rang out. We thought it was one of our party announcing his return. Our three members had stopped to talk with the two from Chicago. We went to investigate the shot which came from south of camp, probably a load shot. Someone was yelling, "Joe. Joe. Joe," and we immediately knew someone was lost, or simply had not returned. We all yelled. No answer, in unison: "JOE! JOE! JOE!"

Again: "JOE, JOE, JOE." We did this for another fifteen minutes and then knew Joe was walking away from us, not toward the camp.

I don't believe either of these fellows knew what time the sun set or how fast it gets dark in the woods once sundown occurs. I decided to attempt to find Joe by hiking back down our trail to the west and by yelling for him. Three of us grabbed flashlights and went about halfway back on our trail calling in vain for Joe. We agreed that we needed assistance from a rescue team and returned to the camp.

We had just made it back to the camp when a rescue team appeared, consisting of several men, an old fire truck, two pickups towing snowmobiles and a couple of cars; they found our "secluded" camp with no difficulty. They had responded with urgency to our call of help.

These people talked with Joe's friend who really couldn't tell them much since he was unfamiliar with the area. One of our gang had a topographical map of the area, showing the location of our camp, which was obviously going to be very helpful. They discussed whether they should use snowmobiles to search for the victim by using the topo map. We assured them there was no way for them to get back into the woods with snowmobiles where the heavy snow had severely bent the small trees and brush down over any trails.

The fire truck was equipped with searchlights, which it directed up into the night like beacons, accompanying the lights with a groaning siren every few minutes. The rescue team stated this technique had been successful previously.

After further assessing the situation, the rescuers asked someone to accompany them to the last stand, which had been mine. I was the only one in the group to have been that far back into the woods in the current conditions so it was decided that I should go. I grabbed my fanny pack (candy bars, matches, T.P., etc.) and left camp with the four rescuers. We took snowmobiles down the road to the trail, but made it less than a hundred yards into the west.

I have a pinned hip from a youthful mishap, which slows me down. This made it extremely difficult to keep pace with the four rescuers, but I kept up, knowing what was at stake. I kept them from veering from the main trails into side trails like those my buddies had taken to their stands, and kept them from following tracks we had made early in the day while blundering around.

Finally we reached my stand. Just before doing so I told the group that we were approaching that goal and pointed out that the only other tracks would be Joe's or those I had made to knock snow off some small trees and brush which had been in my shooting lane.

We approached my stand and right away found Joe's tracks. He had approached the stand, walked right around it, and headed directly northwest. The next road he would encounter would be sixteen miles ahead of him. If he had looked into my stand he would have found my white, five-gallon bucket in which were a small Coleman heater, a space blanket, matches, rope, compass, a sandwich, dry socks, gloves, fire starters, and a flashlight.

At that point I had to part with the rescue team. My hip was hurting and my knee was swollen. I would only be a hindrance to them henceforth. They wouldn't let me leave until being assured I had a flashlight. I dug out my Mini-mag, tested it to show them it worked, and took off for "home" as we called it. I was tired, sore and hungry, and didn't want my flashlight batteries to give out. I tried to keep them warm by wrapping my hand around the case. Not only did I not want the batteries to die, I didn't want to spend the night alone in the woods. When I got back to the camp I was greeted with many thanks for assisting in the rescue attempt. Only one person asked why I had left the team and I told him I had done all I could do.

While I was with the team, all of the people at camp, standing around the fire, joined hands and said a special prayer for Joe, the rescue team, and me, praying that all would return safely.

Within a few minutes we got word that a helicopter would be joining the search in about five minutes. Boy, was it great to hear the sound of that chopper approach, and then to see it.

I should explain that we had three phones in camp, two cellular phones for computer-related calls and one car telephone. We also had one sky pager. All of this because four of us are in the computer business and had lots of equipment available.

The helicopter was equipped with infrared ability, which picks up body heat. It seemed to take a long time for the helicopter to get directly over the area where the ground rescue team was located. The machine had contact with the sheriff and the rescue team back at camp, via citizens' band radio. The sheriff was also assisting, of course.

The helicopter finally located Joe who was about two hundred yards away from the ground rescue team but was moving away from them. Using speakers, the helicopter pilot told Joe to stay where he was and that a rescue team was on its way, but Joe just kept on going. This went on for quite a while, with the ground team gaining on Joe, while all the time Joe kept moving along. When they finally caught up with him, he was about three-quarters of a mile from our camp, in a big swamp. He was exhausted, soaked in icy water up to his armpits, and had no strength to continue. He was on the verge of hypothermia, but the rescue party warmed him up and got him to the south trail where snowmobiles could reach him quite rapidly. That was a much better procedure than trying to backtrack via the search route.

They got him out of the woods at about 10:30 P.M. The rescue team took him away immediately to warm him, to get dry clothing on him, and to get him something warm to eat. We never got to talk to him or learn his friend's name. Each of us wanted to talk with him, but he'd had such a rough time it was felt that he wouldn't remember many details anyhow.

When everyone had left and all had calmed down with only our hunting party sitting around the fire, we discussed the whole incident. We particularly discussed how each of us should always be better prepared and how we could avoid Joe's experience. Even though we were all seasoned hunters and men who knew the rigors of our Minnesota winters, we realized that any one of us lost in the woods, under conditions existing then, could lose his life.

We agreed that none of us would ever enter the woods without the basic items to help save our lives if we became lost or disoriented. And this list would be shared with each new hunter joining our group in the future. We will encourage others to carry the essentials for survival with them every time they go into the woods.

Here is that list of items we demand each of us carry on his person: an extra compass, an extra folding knife, rubber gloves, candy bars, waterproof matches, flares designed to look like rifle casings, a sandwich, a space blanket, a pocket first aid kit, a rope, a small whistler, flashlight, and pop.

This is getting lengthy, but in closing I want to say that I love deer hunting. Taking a deer is a small part of the hunt. It's being up north, in the woods, but best of all its the fellowship. It's being away from the city, away from work, away from the rest of the world. Many people think that deer hunting is only the killing of one of God's creatures. They have to be up north, in the middle of the woods, with the coyotes calling at night. The quiet of the woods, a nice fire burning, and a night when you feel you can see every star. What more can any person want?

GARY JOHNSON
Columbia Heights, Minnesota

Deer Hunting with a Sense of Humor

First thing, I want to inform you that I am deaf; I have been that way since I was four years old and am now in my early seventies. I mention that deafness as a means of humor, which adds to some of my experiences.

In the early fifties, as a recently married young man employed and living in the Fargo, North Dakota–Moorhead, Minnesota, area, I set out one fine fall day on my very first deer hunting foray. A week before the season opened my wife and I had driven up and down country roads near Rollag, Minnesota, which was in reasonable driving distance of our modest apartment in Moorhead. We finally decided on a likely area where there was an opening between two sizeable groves of oak trees—and I had heard that deer were especially fond of acorns. By posting myself at the base of a huge oak tree close to the clearing I'd be well within the range of any deer crossing from one grove to the other. The area was zoned for shotguns with slugs at that time, which made the location of that tree particularly important.

Very early on a Saturday morning a week later, on opening day, I very quietly made my way from the car, which I'd parked back on the road to that lone tree in the middle of the clearing. It was not yet sunrise so I spent time quietly looking for the best spot at the base of that tree, finally leaning back in contentment, but yet alert. Almost immediately I sensed a low vibration and immediately made my gun at ready, expecting a galloping venison-on-the-hoof to break out of one of the groves of trees. But nothing happened.

Right away the vibrations resumed, only this time with more power. Sweat broke out on my brow and my butt tightened in anticipation of something about to happen, but again, nothing moved. Once more these vibrations started and a few leaves even fluttered down onto my shoulder, from above. Then a quick glance upwards revealed a red-clad hunter perched on a limb of my tree high above me. He was angrily gesturing and probably swearing quietly for me to get the heck out of there. The guy had been kicking with his heels and probably knocking against the tree with the butt of his gun to get my attention. By the time we had gotten it all together and had a handshake, it was too late in the morning to go looking for another site. The hunter turned out to be the owner of the land and because it was far off the beaten path, had never posted the land.

Another humorous episode occurred a few years later when I was hunting in the Mahnomen area of Minnesota. I can't remember why I had selected that area but probably someone in the newspaper where I worked mentioned that a lot of big corn and alfalfa-fed deer were in that area and it was not overrun with hunters. I was hunting alone as usual and soon stumbled onto a likely looking fresh deer run and followed it, being sure to keep my distance from the run itself to avoid leaving my scent thereon. Soon I came upon a sizeable aspen which showed signs of having been a deer rub tree quite recently. I stopped by the tree to catch my breath and idly ran my hand over the smooth parts of the rub where the buck's antlers had worn down through the bark, past the cambian layer to the smooth wood underneath. A little farther along I broke into a small clearing where the deer run I was following converged with a deeper run coming from another direction. On the edge of this clearing was a large rotting log which appeared to be an excellent spot to hunker down to await for some unsuspecting buck to come meandering down one of those two trails. The position over by the log seemed to be just perfect, not too far away, and as luck would have it, there was a gentle breeze blowing in my face, downwind of where I would be watching. After a fairly long time, with no movement, I began to relax and began to feel a soft wind blowing on my opened collar. I thought, "Oh, great, now the wind's changed and I'm upwind. Gotta fix that." Turning around to brace myself to get up, I had a big start. Not three feet on the other side of the log was a young spike buck just as startled as I was. He took off with his flag waving in fright, and I didn't recover quickly enough to get a shot off. That young guy must have smelled a little of the buck scent that I had picked up back at the deer run and very quietly came up behind me to snuff me to find out how many points I was sporting on my rack.

A few years later we moved to Alexandria and after a lot of pleading, I was allowed to join my older brother and a group of

his lifelong friends in their annual deer hunting jaunts to northern Minnesota. The bunch jointly owned several hundred acres
of tax-forfeited land up by Pennington, between Cass Lake and
Blackduck. They had put up a cozy fifteen-by-thirty foot one-
room rustic hunting cabin. On the first year I was privy to the
closely knit group, I had a powerful gun, a Winchester .300
Magnum, which handled cartridges almost four inches long. The
first night at the cabin my big gun was passed around to admiration and some ridicule by the guys before finally being handed
back to me by my brother, who remarked, "The rest of us guys
are up here after whitetails and no one can remember ever having
run across any elephant sign." What a kidder. Very early the next
morning as we were filing out past my brother, who was asking
each one of us, "Have you a knife, a rope, matches, toilet paper?"
When it was my turn he asked the usual then asked if I wasn't
forgetting something, then handed me a dishpan from the table.

Noticing my perplexed look, he remarked, "to scoop up all
the hamburger." He was referring to the t remendous damage to
the deer carcass if I hit it with that powerful load. That guy never
let up.

In the end this brother of mine borrowed my big gun to go to
Edmonton, Canada, to bag a moose; a couple of weeks after that
one of the other hunters in our party borrowed the gun to go to
Idaho where he got his big bull elk. So, it was only kidding about
such a big gun, because several of them seemed to be happy that
it was around.

One year a deaf friend from the Twin Cities cajoled me into
letting him come along on a deer hunt with me. It was his very
first deer hunt, in fact, his first time in the big woods. I dropped
him off at a promising stand, beside a likely looking deer run,
and gave him all the necessary instructions about being very, very
quiet, keeping all of his movements at a minimum and asked
him to remain at that spot until I came back for him in a couple
of hours from my station farther up the trail.

He was carrying his brand-new .308 automatic rifle so I figured he might get lucky even if his aim wasn't too good. After a
few hours during which I saw nothing moving, I went back to

pick up my city slicker friend. He was standing in the middle of his clearing in a state of shock. He told me his story.

After the first couple of hours, he just missed having his dream fulfilled. He had been sitting on that stand, moving his eyes back and forth for those two hours, intensely watching the trail. His mind had become mesmerized to all those trees passing past his video and it took several seconds for his mind to register, yes, there was a beautiful deer standing stock still in the middle of his trail, not more than thirty feet directly ahead of him.

In his agitation, he couldn't even raise the tip of his rifle to aim it. It just went *"POW— POW— POW and then a final POW"* right into the ground directly in front of his boots.

Speaking of buck fever, he had really had it.

ROBERT L. CLARK
Alexandria, Minnesota

Nothing to Fear but Fear Itself

One Sunday morning last winter, 1995, three young men from West St. Paul set out on a day hike in Gooseberry Falls State Park on Lake Superior's rugged north shore. They were lightly dressed, having left their jackets behind in the car; the day was mild, and they planned to be gone only for a few hours. They had visited the park on several previous occasions; they carried neither a compass nor a map.

During the day, the young men became confused and lost. On Monday, one of them separated from the others—they had apparently quarreled—and found his way to a snowmobile shelter, which displayed a map of the area. He spent the night there, and the next morning shuffled out to Highway 61, where he was found by a park ranger.

On Wednesday, authorities found the other two young men. One was dead of exposure and exhaustion. The other, found three hundred yards from the body of his friend, was still alive, frostbitten and too weak to move.

The local sheriff would later be criticized for the search effort he led—nobody noticed the boys' car in plain view in one of the park's lots for a full day after they were missing in an area that, although fairly wild, is scarcely remote. And the tragic irony is that such occurrences are not at all uncommon. On the sheriff's first day on the job, just two months earlier, he'd organized the rescue of a Minneapolis man and his seven-year-old son who had strayed in thirty-below-zero weather.

These incidents are grim reminders that any venture into wild country—even country so well trampled as Gooseberry Falls state park—is potentially dangerous, maybe even lethal. That 1995 incident is all the more saddening because it was preventable. If the three young men had simply stayed together and built a big fire, they would almost certainly all still be alive today.

But that is the easy judgment of hindsight. The only good time to think about being lost is before it happens.

The best defense against getting lost is having planned against that possibility. Carry a map and know how to read it, and use it even when you assume you know where you are and where you are headed. [Editor's note: Yes, don't assume. Remember, when you ASSUME you make an ASS out of both U (you) and ME (ASS+U+ME equals ASSUME.)]

Every half-hour or so in unfamiliar country, check to make sure that you and the map agree about where you are. Wear a watch and keep track of the time. As you walk, make mental notes of prominent features of the landscape and remind yourself of them from time to time. They will help you retrace your steps should you become disoriented.

Even if you expect to be gone for only a few hours, carry a day pack. Your emergency supplies should include water, compass, a rain suit, some matches, a few high-energy snack bars, a pocket knife, a loud whistle, a small medical kit, and one of those emergency blankets that weigh only a few ounces. In winter, add an extra set of thermal underwear, a pair of woolen socks, and an extra pair of gloves or mittens.

Sooner or later, if you do enough traveling in wild country, you are going to get lost despite your best precautions. The chief danger in being lost is not in losing your way but in losing your head. You can't, after all, be far from where you intended to be in the first place. The essential features of the landscape haven't gone anywhere. The woods haven't gotten suddenly more threatening, your resources for returning to familiar territory are the same ones you had when you still thought you knew where you were. For all practical purposes, nothing at all has changed except your own state of mind. Take charge of that and you have relatively little to fear.

This, of course, is easier said than done. When your equilibrium has been upset, even tiny events can be discombobulating. Once, alone in the Boundary Waters, I lost my way in a maze of islands on a big lake. I paddled ever more desperately, but nothing I encountered on the lake bore the slightest resemblance to anything on the map before me. It was getting late in the day, so I decided to stop and make camp for the night. The map suggested several possibilities. At dusk I finally reached a very poor campsite and put in.

I pitched my tent on a stony incline and almost immediately went to bed, but it seemed hours before I could doze off. Then, out of the fog of early sleep, I heard some creature sneezing. The sound awakened me like a gunshot. My heart thumped, my palms began to sweat. I swept the pitch darkness with my flashlight but could see nothing. In ordinary circumstances, I would have thought little more of the incident and soon been asleep again, but my nerves were raw. I spent a nearly hysterical night, tossing and turning, staring straight upright at every slight rustle in the forest. When you are in a hypersensitive state, there are a thousand ominous noises in any forest at night.

At the first hint of dawn I was up—and ready for a straightjacket. Fortunately it was one of those magical September mornings when a dreamy fog rises from glassy waters. I brewed myself a big pot of tea, slobberingly grateful to have lived to see another day, and gradually my peace of mind returned. I got out my map when I was calm again and studied it carefully. It did not matter, I saw, whether I knew precisely where I was. If I simply set a compass heading due south and paddled until I reached the shore of the lake and then followed the shoreline in a clockwise direction, I would sooner or later have to reach the portage for which I was searching.

An hour later I had found it. The solution ought to have been perfectly obvious all along, but not until I had control of my emotions was I able to think of it.

The worst danger when you think you might be lost is self-delusion. Forget intuition at such a moment. There is no such thing as an innate sense of direction. Don't make hasty assumptions. In a certain frame of mind you can make your eyes see anything you want them to see.

Last summer, again alone, I was hiking a remote section of the Continental Divide in Montana. I was following a long-abandoned Jeep trail still faintly discernible in the forest but indecipherably overgrown in the meadow openings. It had been a tedious morning of maddeningly confused pathfinding. Finally, well after noon, I came to the established pack trail that I had been aiming for. I reached it at a fork, as I expected, that fork being clearly marked on my map. The problem was it was not at all obvious which of the forks I should take. Both led off ambiguously in more or less the same direction. I shed my backpack, explored both alternatives for a quarter of a mile, studied my maps, took various compass readings, and still the choice was not clear.

I had a general description of the terrain I was to cross. (I was test-walking a proposed rerouting of the Continental Divide trail.) I knew that I was to head down a mountainside to the valley of a major stream, crossing along the way a couple of its minor branches; that I would pass through a beaver meadow; that I would cross a wooden footbridge; that eventually I would reach a road passable by car; and that down that road I would find a Forest Service campground. I also knew that my route was generally downhill to the west and south. There were enough details so that, were I to choose the wrong fork initially, this would soon, I told myself, be apparent.

With that reassurance and no better idea about how to proceed, I chose the fork in the trail that felt right. And indeed all of the appropriate landmarks appeared approximately where I expected to find them. I crossed minor branches of a stream, spent the night in a beaver meadow, crossed a wooden bridge the next day, came to a road passable by car, followed it, and eventually reached a Forest Service campground, where I spent the next night. From where I believed myself to be it was only a few miles to a village which was said to have an excellent restaurant and a telephone. I planned to laze around the town for a day, gorge myself on real food, and call my family.

Because the town was such a short distance from my campsite, I had a leisurely breakfast and even washed a few clothes before setting out. It was blazingly hot, at least a hundred degrees. I walked and walked and walked. Sometimes anticipation makes the short days on a trail seem harder than the long ones, I reminded myself. At about five o'clock that afternoon I passed a ranch. I walked another hundred yards, and then doubled back. The sign read, "Blackfoot River Ranch." I knew to my immediate dismay, that I should have been far south of the Blackfoot

river. It was hard to believe, but unarguably true—it became
clear when I consulted my maps—that I had just spent three
days backpacking some fifty miles north and east rather than
south and west. I had gone disastrously astray, and I had only the
most general notion of my whereabouts.

I sat down dazed at the edge of the road. I felt like crying, but
I didn't see that it would help. As I have trained myself to do—
being lost was not, I am, chagrined to admit, a new experience
for me—I thought carefully about my alternatives. It did not
take long; there was really only one choice. With a heart nearly as
heavy as my tired feet, I shouldered my pack and began, one
awful step at a time, to retrace every inch of the previous fifty
miles. I covered the ground in two days rather than three the second time around, getting a bit angrier at myself by the hour.

I had plenty of time to reconstruct what had gone wrong. As
I thought about it, I realized that I had had about a hundred
solid clues—including such neon-red flags as the orientation of
the sun and the readings on my compass, that should have
alerted me that I was headed in the wrong direction. I have
walked thousands of wilderness miles. It was not as if I didn't
know better. But I so wanted the choice I had made at that trail
junction to be the right one that I had rationalized away or ignored every contrary item of information that my addled brain
had received.

My hundred-mile detour in a direction completely opposite
from the one intended was a bitter reminder that one should always mistrust intuition in the wilderness. Assume nothing and
you can never make a false assumption.

When you realize that you are lost, the first thing to do is
nothing at all. Stop. Sit down, take a nap, make yourself a sandwich, photograph some flowers, sing camp songs, recite
poems—do anything that will take your mind off your predicament until you are able to think calmly and clearly. A rushed person afoot in the wild is almost certain to rush in the wrong direction, and haste is the surest way to become even more lost than
you already are. If it is cold, build a fire. If it is raining, build
some kind of shelter. If it is morning, wait until after lunch to

contemplate your next move. If it is past noon and you are not on a day hike, hunker down where you are, set up camp, and spend the night. Your options will be clearer in the morning.

Either way, calm down and then think through your situation systematically. Limit your thinking strictly to the visible evidence. Think back to the last point where you were confident of your whereabouts. If you have a map, mentally retrace your route from where you started to that point and mark it.

How fast were you walking? Two miles an hour is the average pace for most hikers. How long have you been walking since you left the place you have marked on the map? If it has been two hours, assume that you are within four miles of that point. On the map draw a radius of four miles around it. You are probably within the confines of that circle.

Now look at the terrain surrounding you. Are you on high ground or low ground? In forest or in the open? On flat ground or on a slope? In what direction were you traveling when you realized you were lost? Where is the sun? If there is no sun or it is too high in the sky to orient you, think about the basic features of the landscape. What is the general orientation of the ridges or rivers in this part of the country? Perhaps there is a climbable tree nearby that would afford you a view of the terrain. Have you been walking up and down ridges, following the drainage of a river, or contouring a hill? What does this suggest about the direction in which you were probably traveling?

Did you pass by any feature of the landscape that might show on the map: a lake or pond, a hill or ridge, a stream or river, a footpath, an opening in the woods? If you can remember such a feature, try to find it within the circle on the map. If you can do so and it lies in the direction you were traveling when you realized you were lost, you now have a solid clue as to your whereabouts. By studying the map and thinking carefully about your movements since you saw that feature of the landscape, can you make a reasonable guess about where you are now? If you can, you are ready to plan a way out.

Your best choice—if it's feasible—is to go back the way you came. Otherwise, set your sights on the nearest road or trail.

How can you get to it? What features of the landscape ought to be visible along the way?

Before setting off, rethink your strategy one final time. If your plan seems reasonable on review, you're ready to move. Now is the time for religious use of your compass, if you have one. Remember: Once you have figured out where you are and how to make a safe return, it is still possible to get lost once again on your way out. Set a course on the map, and follow the compass closely, no matter what your instincts tell you to the contrary. If your instincts were worth following you wouldn't be lost. Even if your assumptions about your location turn out to be wrong, a straight-line course will sooner or later lead you to someplace you can recognize on a map.

But suppose you have been foolhardy and are carrying neither a compass nor a map. Your situation is more difficult, but it is not impossible.

It is wintertime and there is snow on the ground; follow your tracks.

If you are on or near a river or creek, find it and follow it downstream.

If you have been walking uphill, go downhill.

If you are on a trail system in a park and have become confused, the system undoubtedly makes a loop. Set out in any direction, and, whenever you come to an intersection, always take the right-hand alternative. This will probably not be the shortest way back to your starting point, but it will get you there.

With even the most modest skills, you can at least get yourself to a road. You can do that by walking in a straight line until you come to one. Count on such a walk to take at least twice as long as you think it ought to. Remember how long an hour in the car seemed when you were a kid? When you're eager to get somewhere and are at the mercy of forces beyond your control, time drags.

This is how you walk in a straight line without a compass. Choose the tallest landmark in your immediate vicinity and fix it in your mind. Choose another landmark several hundred yards ahead. Walk to it. Choose a third landmark in line with the first two and walk to it, repeating this exercise proceeding from point to point, until you come to a road. If the road is signed and you recognize it, follow it to help. Otherwise, wait there for the assistance of a passing motorist.

Here are some situations in which you should not try to walk to safety. Don't set out if you are seriously injured, you're feeling panicky, if you are exhausted, or if it is snowing, raining hard, or foggy, particularly if you are not properly dressed to withstand exposure to them.

In such circumstances, your safest alternative is to wait where you are to be found. Your strategy should be to make yourself as conspicuous as possible. Get into the open if the landscape and the weather conditions allow it. The first search for you is likely to be made by air. If you have a brightly colored scrap of cloth, make a flag and raise it. Start a fire and keep it going. Stay put.

If you are in a group, stay together. The more of you there are, the more likely you are to be spotted, and the more resources for survival you'll have. This will take some formal discipline since everybody's nerves will be frayed. Designate the calmest and most experienced member of your group as the leader.

If there is some evidence of a search—if you see an airplane overhead, for instance, or hear voices—do your best to raise a commotion, but don't waste your energy unless there is solid reason to believe that you might be seen or heard. Keep as warm and dry as possible. Find a source of water if you can. You can survive for a long time without food but not without water. Try to get some sleep. If you can calm down enough to doze off, you've overcome the panic that is your biggest potential problem.

This is not the time for heroics. Somebody is undoubtedly looking for you. Your job is to stay alive until you are found. In the worst of circumstances your ordeal is not likely to last longer than two or three days.

You might even find that, in retrospect, being lost was not an ordeal at all, but an adventure. I can still feel the sheer joy I knew that morning in the Boundary Waters when I discovered the portage I had been looking for. And I cherish the memory of that beaver meadow in Montana. I watched the beavers there as they went about their evening repairs of the dams, so unwary as to be oblivious to my presence, and I watched a magnificent bull moose grazing among a pad of water lilies in bloom, and in the middle of the night a mountain lion screamed twice, its cries rolling off the mountainsides. I walked almost a thousand miles through the heart of the Montana Rockies and never heard a more thrilling sound or saw a more beautiful place. Had I not been lost, I would never have found it.

PAUL GRUCHOW
Northfield, Minnesota

Young Huntress Decides
Deer Hunting Not for Her

When our youngest daughter, Debbie, was ten years old, we enrolled her in a local high school gun safety course. She was the only girl among the fifteen other students. The instructor, Patrolman Dave Benson of our city's police force, was a family friend familiar with our outdoors-oriented family and readily accepted the girl in the course. After Debbie had completed the course and we had framed and hung up her certificate, we presented her with grandpa's old .22-calibre rifle. Throughout the summer Debbie and her father were forever roaming the woods and lakeshores plinking at targets and communing with nature in other ways.

Early in the fall the two went squirrel hunting and after a time, when Debbie was getting more squirrels than her old man, it was decided to introduce her to the more exciting sport of hunting upland game birds and waterfowl.

It soon became apparent that this young girl didn't care for this heavy shotgunning but was forever hinting that her father should take her deer hunting when that season rolled around. So, on her twelfth birthday, we bought her a light deer rifle, an ideal gun for a beginner. It had reach and pretty good killing power, and it's recoil was light.

That fall Debbie accompanied me and Bob up north on our private deer hunt; we were hunting on Bob's brother's private land, and Bob not only was very familiar with the land but already had an ideal spot picked for a stand for Debbie. It was an elevated stand overlooking a natural salt lick area which had been there for years.

After helping her into the stand and giving her all the last-minute instructions she could possibly need, we moved farther down from the stand but not so far away that we could not observe what was happening. It is important to know that Debbie could "sign" and lip read, since both of her parents are hearing impaired; Debbie, however, has normal hearing.

For most of the morning, we were conversing back and forth in sign language, that being soundless, of course.

Then suddenly Debbie went rigid, staring down right into the frightened brown eyes of a beautiful young doe, which appeared out of nowhere and was ankle-deep in nature's salt lick.

Debbie signaled, "Deer down there," while Bob was signaling back, "Shoot! Shoot! Shoot!.

Debbie just stood there on the stand, shaking her head, mouthing, "I can't. I just can't. She's too pretty." By this time the young doe decided it was time to hightail it out of there. Bob didn't even try for her, although she was easily within the range of his rifle. He didn't want Debbie to see the kill either, thinking it might sour her on the sport.

Later in the afternoon Bob downed a young buck at another site and field dressed it there before dragging it back to the cabin where we were waiting.

By this time Debbie had her emotions under control and came outside to examine the carcass. We had the hide from this deer tanned with the hair on and presented it to her as a souvenir of her first deer hunt, but although she treasures that beautiful deer skin, she never asked to go with us again. A few years later she asked if it was okay to sell her unused gun and buy a good camera. She had decided her future hunting days would be with camera instead of rifle. So it took only one fleeting look at a young deer to sour our huntress daughter on all forms of hunting.

Maycel Clark
Alexandria, Minnesota

Eye-to-Eye with a Big Buck

The morning was like any other frozen one, except for the crank of the alarm at 4:00 A.M. instead of at a more reasonable hour. Everyone else was asleep, and the stairs just had to creak as my younger brother, Tory, and I made our way up to the kitchen. It was opening day of the 1995 deer season so getting up before the dog came easy. We enjoyed a bowl of cereal, and I made the usual thermos of hot chocolate for the afternoon. This was my brother's first hunt and he eventually put on the clothes I had picked out for him the night before. He looked like the Michelin Man at the time, and I wasn't sure I was going to take him in the morning or return for him later that afternoon. But this morning I felt I should take him, partly because I remembered how I felt being told "No" when I wanted to go at his years.

After the polypropylene was on and we had gone to the bathroom one last time, I said it was time to go; I could tell that Tory was getting warm with anticipation, so we picked up my bag and gun and headed out the door. I had decided to hunt in back of the house this year because of all the signs I had seen there.

We walked down the neighbor's drive because there's a good 120 acres of private land there. I really didn't have a specific spot in mind but we walked until we got to the pipeline and then went back to a spot I thought about. I knew where the deer were crossing in the morning, which was only about three-fourths of a mile away. The land is rough and rolling and there is a watering hole at the bottom of one of the hills, with the land coming to a four-way stop at the pond. Woods were on each side with the pond in the middle. We headed for the top of the hill to the left of the pond where the pipeline split two large stands of oak trees. The area is fairly clear of underbrush, but it gets thick farther in the woods. I didn't have a stand up there so was taking my chances sitting on the ground. I found a good tree and told Tory to sit there while I put out scent cannisters around us. I was set up on the backside of the hill overlooking the swamp into which the deer are funneled. At the top of the next hill the pipeline crossed a power line, forming a good shooting area. I could see a good distance in all directions, so I was feeling excited about the day to come.

About 6:15 I sat down to wait. The soft dusting of snow on the leaves would help give me an earful if anything were moving. After about ten minutes of shooting light, I could hear them coming and told Tory to look with his eyes, not his body. I sat there anticipating what was coming for about five minutes before I saw them. Two dogs! What? Dogs? They came running right up the hill toward Tory and me. I was set up just perfectly and here came those two animals to investigate. If it hadn't been for the fact that Tory was with me, and because of my soft spot, those dogs might have had their last run.

They finally left without even knowing Tory and I were even there. I prayed they wouldn't influence the deer movement that morning. This was Tory's first deer hunt; he was fresh out of gun safety class and wanted to be like his brother—and I truly hoped he'd have a great experience. Although he wasn't carrying a gun, that didn't matter to him, because he was still hunting. And learning.

As the sun melted the frost on the trees, we both began to get a chill from the wind which was picking up. I told Tory to curl up and close his eyes, and I would tell him if I saw anything coming. It was now about 8:00 A.M. and I was getting knots in my back from the cold and my awkward position on the ground. There was nothing moving except birds and my hands were cold knots inside my gloves. I figured if nothing moved it was time to make some noise. Rattle, a good way to keep warm, and maybe bring in a deer. So I pulled out my antlers and grunt tube and went at it. I crashed those things together so hard I thought I would awaken the neighbors in the crispness of the morning. Then a grunt, a single grunt! Something had heard me and was responding.

I continued this sequence for about twelve minutes and decided to rest. In about seven more minutes the woods came alive. I heard a rustle/crunch across the pipeline to my right in the thicker brush, and then I saw what I had heard. I told Tory to sit still and that I thought a deer was coming in. I stood up and saw a brown back moving away from us. I grunted again and he stopped. I say "he" because when he stopped and turned I saw antlers in the sun. I told Tory who immediately said, "Shoot him."

I grunted again until I knew I had his attention. He crossed the pipeline and picked up my scent trail. That's when I really became a believer in scents. His nose was right on the ground. I was still standing directly behind the birch tree where I had been sitting all the time, so I had to peek around the corner to see him coming. Here he came, walking in the same tracks Tory and I had used to get to our stand. He was in our very tracks.

I was getting that feeling inside, when your heart beats faster and your ears feel funny. This deer was only spitting distance away, maybe twenty yards, and coming closer. He was walking slowly, taking his time, eyeballing for the other deer he expected to see.

I had never watched a buck this close for so long. He came closer and stopped directly across from me; he looked right at me. I mean he stared me down. I could see the nervousness in his eyes. My gun wasn't up because the tree was in the way; I pulled up my gun and shouldered it, standing very still. I didn't even breathe lest he see my frozen breath and run. He did a couple of head circles, apparently thinking something wasn't quite right, then wheeled and trotted up the hill. Boy, did I worry that I had lost him. Then he stopped, turned broadside, and walked into a perfect shot for me. I shouldered the gun, waited until he stopped, and lined up my shot.

Tory was telling me, "Shoot. Shoot. Shoot." I agreed and put the sights in back of his right quarter and squeezed the trigger.

My 30-06 answered with a thump, and in the shadow of the sun I saw the hair blow back upon the impact of the shot. I had made a good shot and immediately knew it.

I grabbed Torey to keep him from running up there in case the buck wasn't dead, as I chambered another shell just in case.

I was shaking with that feeling we all know. We waited five minutes and we approached the spot, with me insisting Tory keep behind me.

No blood. Instant panic. Impossible that I missed. We looked around for a while, and there he was. Out cold. He had taken no more than two steps and fell over. The shot was thirty yards at the most. My bullet had kissed his heart and one lung.

I called Tory over and, boy, was he excited. The deer had eight points—no, seven, because one of the brow tines was broken. Nice rack. Not a Boone & Crockett, but a good deer to have at 8:33 on opening morning.

I had never shot a dceer that early on opening morning and I was rather sad it was all over so soon. I can't complain, though. I got what I wanted, what I came for, and it was a hunt we'll never forget. This was the first one with my little brother and I knew it wouldn't be the last. He told all of his friends about it and we even made the local newspaper, as bringing in the first registered buck of the season, a two hundred-pound buck.

I hope the next time it will be Tory's deer we can talk about.

Tom Cawcutt
Carlton, Minnesota

My First Deer – At Age Twelve

"Brian, Brian. It's time to get up."

I slowly opened my eyes, yawned and pulled the blanket up over me, realizing how cold I was sleeping on the couch. I wondered "Why do I do this to myself?" I get up at 5 A.M., cold, tired, and crabby. Then I eat, dress, and go sit in a stand, listening to other people off in the distance, listening to the squirrels laugh at me, freeze half to death, get down, hike a mile or two home, go downstairs and unlayer myself of excess clothes, then go have a piece of Grandma's cherry pie.

I'm twelve years old and this was my first year of hunting, the second day of deer hunting in 1986. We were skunked the first day so were going to try it again, meaning my grandpa, dad, sister, uncle, his partner, and me.

My dad took my older sister to their stands while my uncle Mark took his partner to their stands to hunt. I had gone with my dad yesterday and we saw nothing. Today my grandfather said he'd take me and show me how to hunt.

If anyone is going to show me how to get a deer, it would be my grandpa. He's done it for about seventy years and I don't think he has ever been skunked. We took his four-wheeler three-quarters of a mile into the woods and we walked across the grade fifty yards to our stand at about 6 A.M. We got settled in the one stand, Grandpa looking north, me looking south. We had carpet around the stand to protect us from the wind and a charcoal heater to protect us from the cold, so we were good for all day. The woods looked nice with a little snow on the trees, a couple of chickadees chirping, and a couple of squirrels laughing at us. I threw little pine needles in the fire to hear them snap; I looked up and saw a doe walking along the grade.

I pointed it out to my grandpa who said, "Shoot it." "No", I said, "I don't have a doe permit and neither do you." He looked at me like I'm overcome with buck fever, takes his old 348, aims. (I plug my ears) and BOOM the whole tree stand shakes. I look up to see the doe fall over sideways and also to see a buck, who was following her, now run away. "I saw a buck", I yelled and started down. Now it doesn't matter where you hit a deer with a

348, that deer is going down and I was positive Grandpa's doe was dead. My grandpa said, "Forget it, he's gone." So we got down and dressed Grandpa's doe, then dragged it into the bush. Grandpa told me to go back up in the stand while he went to Mark's stand where we had also heard a shot.

While he was gone, I played with the little heater and burned a hole in my clothes. Twenty minutes later Grandpa returned and told me Mark got a fourteen-point buck. There goes my dream buck, I thought. Darned it. I might as well get down and go back to the cities. Once again Grandpa left with the four-wheeler and I was left alone up in the stand with the heater.

He returned fifteen minutes later without the four-wheeler because my uncle needed it to drag in his buck. Then my grandpa said he was going to make a drive for me. So he walked down the grade a bit and turned into the woods.

I was looking at where the doe was shot when suddenly all the squawking squirrels and birds shut up—just as if turned off. I turned around and saw a huge ten-pointer coming my way. My eyes almost popped out of my head and I stood up for some dumb reason, making all kinds of noise. The big buck looked up, snorted, and trotted a little faster; at the time I thought he was too big to run. I grabbed my 30-06, aimed, closed my eyes, and squeezed the trigger. Then I felt something hit me in the eye super hard. It was my scope—my head was too close to the gun,

But I got that huge buck.

I looked up to see the buck using its front hooves trying to get up. I squeezed off another shot, which just made the hole in his ribs bigger, then got off two more shots, hitting him in the same place all the time slowing him down, while trying to be careful of the antlers. I shot at the neck with my last cartridge and broke its antler off. It was now dead.

I went down to look at it and my grandpa came out of the woods, saw the big hole in its back, and said, "Oh, Hell." He was swearing to himself and I was thinking to myself, "But I got it, didn't I?"

Everyone I talked to said they would have kept shooting, too. But some said it was buck fever, while others said it was brains.

To remember its size, I stretched out my pinky and thumb on

one hand, made a fist with the other hand, put them together, and that's how far apart the tip of the rack was. My grandpa and I had a hard time dragging that old buck over the weeds back to the camp, but it was worth it.

I'll never forget the day my grandpa helped me get my first buck.

BRIAN J. ANDERSON
Bloomington, Minnesota

Guess Who Gets to Clean It?

I had the opportunity to attend the annual Whitetail show of the Minnesota Deer Hunter's Association, held in suburban Minneapolis in February 1996. There I witnessed the astounding interest by young boys and men, as well as their seniors, in an exhibit of hunting with a laser-powered rifle. Set up as a demonstration model of how such a rifle could be used as a training tool on a range or even as owned by a gun club, it also proved to be a magnet for the young boys who wanted to test their ability with something more than an air rifle or a .22-caliber gun. Those males (and a few females) who were permitted to test their skills were also learning some safety skills at the same time. To me, it was obviously more than just a chance to show a product, hoping to make a sale to a club or a range owner. Since I was exhibiting there myself, attempting to make contact with deer hunters from whom I could learn some good stories for this book, it was a pleasant surprise to receive this letter a couple of weeks later— William H. Hull

It was a Sunday evening in November in my thirteenth year. It was the very last day of the deer season and my hunting party had been skunked for the whole season. Not one of the five of us had downed a deer; not my grandpa, not my uncle, not my two cousins, not me.

It was about 3:00 P.M. and I was dressed in my bright orange snowmobile suit, had my loaded lever-action 30-30 Winchester, took a grateful breath of that clean country air, and started for my deer stand.

As time passed I sat there like the traditional bump on a log, just waiting for something to happen. Finally I heard something through the woods moving toward me. Then something caught my eye; it was about twenty yards away and at first I thought it might be a rabbit eating or browsing. But then it moved out from behind the brush and it was a full-sized deer.

A deer!

My stomach started to turn and twist like a rag being twisted to remove the water from it. It felt dry as if there were nothing in it.

So I clicked back the hammer; the deer stood still and I pulled the trigger. The deer started to run toward me, which was a surprise. As I quickly reloaded, the deer turned away from me and I shot a second time. Then I quickly reloaded again and shot the third time, but the shot hit a tree. My fourth and last shot hit a tree beside him as he went running off into the woods. I didn't get another chance as I saw him running off through the timber.

I went to get my grandpa to get his help to see if I had him and could track him down the trail.

As we tracked the deer we soon started to find some blood, and there, at about 150 yards from the stand, we found my eight-point buck, my very first deer.

My grandpa said, "You did real good, very good".

It was now getting dark in the woods, too dark to see well, so we dragged him back to the barn, at which time my Grandpa said, "Guess who gets to clean him out"?

Nick Gross
Maple Grove, Minnesota

That Huge Horse Charged Right at Me

I started deer hunting when I was twenty-one years old, fresh out of the Marine corps.

I found my military skills were no match for the elusive whitetail, as I hunted for seven years without even seeing a deer. Although everyone else in the party would see deer, I never did. I read everything I could find about deer hunting, descented my clothes, scouted the territory in advance of the season, but during the season I never saw hide nor hair of a deer.

I thought I was jinxed until I saw the horse in the woods.

I was sitting on an old stump, being very still, when about seventy-five yards in front of me I saw a roan-colored horse. Immediately I thought, "What the heck is a horse doing in the woods in northern Minnesota?" It was brownish-red or roan in color and was walking with its head down, grazing on the forest floor. A horse!

Then I caught a glint of light on its head. Those were *antlers!* It's a deer. I said to myself, "A horse doesn't have horns." It was a huge deer.

But it was the wrong color. I raised the 30-06 and put the iron sights on the vital area behind the right foreleg, and pulled the trigger. The horse-deer turned and bolted toward me at full gallop, getting bigger and bigger coming straight at me, charging me with its head down. I noticed it was blowing blood with each exhale and fired again into its chest. I heard the bullet "slap," but on it came, now less than fifty yards away. I cocked another round and fired again. "Splat," I heard the round smack his chest.

On it came, now thirty yards away. He lowered his head. Somehow I fired two more offhand shots, but this time through my barrage I heard him snorting and blowing blood. Then, just as I was about to be run over by this red "horse" it dropped at my feet, barely inches away — dead.

My first shot had hit him in the lungs, the other four all hitting him in the chest with a group the size of a silver dollar. My Marine drill instructor would have been proud of my small group and unwavering fire discipline. When a deer is charging you there's no place to run, or no time to do anything but stand your ground and fire. What a surprise, a horse that turned into a deer! It just shows how your mind can play tricks on you when you are in the woods.

This particular year there was no snow, and when I wrapped my rope around his antlers and tried to drag him out, I could only move it three or four feet at a time. Then a couple of hunters came along and helped me drag it. One of these hunters said he had been hunting for forty years and had never seen a deer that large or that color.

We finally got the animal loaded in my VW bus, where it filled the whole compartment.

It dressed out at 248 pounds with a twelve-point rack.

Now that I know what they look like, I've gotten one nearly every year since.

ROBERT DYBEVIK
Prior Lake, Minnesota

Downed a 206-Pound Buck with a 410 Shotgun

My most memorable deer hunt happened in Carver County on November 7, 1973, about the time the deer started to come back to the agricultural land. Prior to that we always went up north to do our deer hunting.

The night before the deer season opened I happened to be doing some field work as it was getting dark. I looked out over the neighbor's freshly picked cornfield and saw a large animal on his field. I thought that one of his steers was out, but upon closer examination, I realized it was a deer.

Deer fever set in very quickly.

I jumped into my brand-new 1973 Ford truck and went to town to get my license and shotgun shells. What a disappointment to find they didn't have any twelve guage slugs left, because I owned a twelve-gauge automatic gun.

I did, however, have shells with slugs for my 410-gauge single shotgun. The problem was it had no front sight. The BB had been broken off and, besides, it was a hammer-type gun bought used when I was a youngster in 1942 for pheasant hunting.

Early the next morning when deer season opened I was waiting behind a big tree on the long hill next to the willow swamp. When it finally got light enough to see, I looked in the direction of the neighbor's cornfield.

Sure enough! There was this big deer eating corn left on the ground, about a fourth of a mile away.

It seemed forever, but he finally came closer, following the hill down to the swamp where I waited.

With the northwest wind blowing and my eyes watering and waiting with my 410 single shot gun, it seemed like eternity before that big deer walked closer and closer along the bottom of the hill. When he was directly below me, at about seventy-five feet, I shot, knowing it had to be now or never, a once-in-a-lifetime chance to tell my grandchildren a true story about deer hunting. The big buck dropped down. With that front sight gone my shot was high and it hit the spine. He didn't move again.

Now what? My wife was still sleeping as was the whole family. I drove home, the two and a half miles, awoke my wife and told her she should get dressed and help me load a big deer I had just shot. As she looked at me I could see what she was thinking, "You must be crazy but just this one time I'll do it."

The ten-point buck tipped the scales at 206 pounds and was the best cornfed deer meat I ever tasted. One of the prongs was broken off due to fighting or whatever, but the antlers adorn our den and bring back memories from a long time ago.

If I had to do it again I would have awakened my four-year-old son and taken him along when we got the deer at seven in the morning because now when I tell this story, he gives me that look. Is that how it was?

RUBEN SCHUMACHER
Mayer, Minnesota

Rookies' First Try

It started on a late summer afternoon when I stopped at a local sports shop just to look at the new fall gear and happened to see a moose hunt license application while the clerk was ringing up my order. The application for posting a permit needed to be postmarked that very day. It was deadline time.

Since moose hunting season is held on alternate years here in Minnesota and the permit application requires four hunters, I had to move fast. With three friends I had applied the last two seasons but had not been lucky enough to draw a permit.

As rookies, *our first mistake was that we should have been aware of deadlines ahead of time.*

I raced home to start calling my hunting friends but could reach only two of them, Dan and Paul, and told them I had an application and to stop by and sign it. They both showed up around 4:00 and signed. We knew we had to be very careful when filling out the application because one little error can cause it to be rejected by the DNR. We spent almost an hour studying the map, checking on the number of permits allowed in each zone, but none of us had ever hunted these areas before. We tried to contact our fourth friend, Ron, but we couldn't reach him. Finally, we learned from his wife that he was out of town but would be returning about 8:00. We told her that he had to stop by my house to sign and help make decisions. I was about ready to sign his name and mail the form when he called at 10:30 and said he would arrive in about fifteen minutes, having had some truck problems.

Sure enough, he arrived soon and signed the application, after which we took about twenty minutes to decide where to hunt. We finally made a selection, jumped into the truck, and rushed to the main post office in downtown Minneapolis where we found all the main doors locked. We thought surely one would be open for people like us who wait until the last minute. When we were about to give up we spotted two other guys rushing in with a package. They told us to go to the dock area in the rear of the post office and sometimes a guard would get it postmarked. We rushed there and the truck wasn't at a complete stop when I was out the door and running as fast as I could, to grab the first guard and ask him if he could get our letter postmarked by midnight. He looked at his watch; it was 11:55 and asked what was so important that it had to be postmarked that quickly. When I told him it was our moose application, he grabbed the letter and took off running, yelling over his back, "You're damned right I will get it postmarked. I'm a hunter, too." We waited for him to return so we could thank him, but we never saw him again and left, wondering if he had gotten it postmarked on time.

Summer came to an end and it was getting into early fall. The thought of getting a moose license had almost faded from my memory. One afternoon my wife called me at work to tell me there was a big surprise waiting for me at home. She wouldn't tell me anymore but, like a small child, the day dragged on until I could go home. I rushed home to find my wife with my gun case in her hands with a letter from the DNR taped to it. I tore open the envelope and excitedly read, *"You and your party are the proud owners of a Minnesota moose license."*

I called my three hunting friends to share the good news. Of course, each one had to come over to see the good news with his own eyes. The first thing Ron asked was, "Which area did we pick?" None of us could remember because of the stress of trying to get it postmarked that night. Finally I could tell them it was east of Thief River Falls.

So, like they say in some other sports, we "had made the cut."

We were going moose hunting!

Two weeks before the season was to open we decided we needed to scout our hunting area. We left town Saturday morning around 2:00 A.M. It's about a six-hour drive to our area. We stopped at several farmhouses and talked to the owners of the land about a place to camp and different places we could hunt. We drove around for four hours, checking the area. We saw four moose, one a huge bull. We stopped back at the farm where we were going to camp to talk to the farmer about moose hunting. The farmers in that area hate moose. That man said moose are so dumb they would come right up to the tractor while farmers were working the fields. He said they didn't use normal cattle fences because the moose would get their antlers or feet caught in them and just keep on going, breaking the wood fence posts right off. They used electric wire, which was cheaper to repair. He said if the moose got caught in the electric fence it would sometimes pull up a quarter of a mile of the fence. The electricity didn't bother them at all.

He told us the only way to hunt moose was to drive around until you see one and then shoot it. We were told this by other area residents also.

We left the north country, feeling confident that getting a moose would be easy, just like shooting a cow. How could anyone not be able to see a moose? Minnesota has over a 90 percent kill rate for moose season.

Rookie mistake #2: Get professional advice on moose hunting. Attend a DNR moose hunting class.

We did a lot of preseason planning and preparation. We made a backpack which contained knives, saws, axes. and cloth bags in which we might have to put moose quarters, rope, plastic tarps in case of rain, tent stakes, canvas tarps to help in moving the moose out of the woods, plastic gloves and many other items. We left town the Friday before the opening at anbout 5:00 A.M. in Ron's 1978 Chevy diesel station wagon. We thought it would be a lot cheaper to go in one vehicle.

Rookie mistake #3. We should have taken two vehicles, one being a heavy four-wheel drive, preferably.

We arrived at our campsite at 1:00 P.M. and immediately set up the big tent and got our camp in order. We then drove around to locate most of the action. We were not a quarter of a mile away from our camp when a big cow moose ran across the road right in front of us, causing us to come to a complete stop to avoid hitting it. We thought, "Dumb moose. See you tomorrow." We continued driving around for three hours and saw two other moose at a distance. Our hopes were high as we awaited the coming sunrise.

We were up two hours before sunrise because none of us could sleep that night. We had a good breakfast, made sandwiches, and filled the cooler with cans of pop. We drove all day long, about 250 miles, without seeing a thing. We drove on dirt roads, gravel roads, trails, and even on the main highway, stopping every two hours to stretch our legs. We decided to return to camp where we had seen the cow moose the day before. We spent the last hour of daylight waiting for the cow, but she never appeared. Later that night we found out why. Another farmer, neighbor of the man on whose land we were camped, had been driving by his field at sunrise that morning and that same moose walked right up to the road. He jumped out of the car and shot it, just ten minutes into the season.

DAMN! It was the same farmer who had told us to drive around all day. We were in the right spot but at the wrong time.

We awoke about sunrise, not quite as excited as on the day before. We knew it was going to be a long day. We decided to drive the area where we had seen the big bull on our preseason trip. It took about an hour to drive to that area, and we were driving along a curving road when we noticed tracks on the road. Or were they? None of us had ever seen moose tracks and walked down the road following the tracks. Dan suddenly mentioned, "Hey, we don't have any guns with us." We were so excited to see those tracks that we had walked away from our guns.

Suddenly, out of nowhere came this pickup. It came to a fast stop at our tailgate and out jumped two game wardens with their hands on their guns, one on each side of the car.

"Out of the car, right now!" they yelled.

We all got out. They asked to see each of our cased guns, one at a time. Boy, were we happy that we had obeyed the law and our guns were cased and not loaded. They asked to see our licenses. Mine wasn't signed so they made me sign it. They looked in the car for other guns or maybe booze. I believe they thought they had stopped us for something illegal. But we explained; we were inexperienced moose hunters, hunting as we were told to do. They left, wishing us good luck, but saying, "There are a lot better ways to hunt moose." We gave up the chase when the moose tracks went into a big swamp.

We decided to drive to the south end of our area, which we had not covered before. That area was more open than the north end with more fields and farms. We were driving on a gravel road when again we spotted tracks along the side of the road. This time we looked in back of us to see if we were being followed

(DNR). We were not going to be stopped again. The tracks led along the edge of the field, so we decided to spread out on the opposite side of the field. We had been standing along this edge for about an hour when we heard something coming out of the woods. That noise was coming from the far corner of the field, right where the tracks had led. The noise kept getting louder — and closer. Suddenly, out came three milk cows driven by a local farm kid. Rookies!

We decided to go hunt our first area. When we were about two miles from our camp we found a new dirt road leading into what looked to be a nice, quiet hunting spot, with no milk cows around. We decided that, after driving for almost two days, it was time to change our hunting method. We decided to do some walking, so we drove back to the road for about a mile, then had to stop. The Corps of Engineers was working on a flood control project and had the road blocked to traffic. We paired up and headed in different directions: Paul and I headed east while Ron and Dan went west. We walked along the ditch but couldn't get across to the other side. We climbed onto a big dirt pile to see if there was any way we could make it to the other side. There was a clear-cut on the other side which looked as if it had been made for a fire break. It was about a hundred yards across and about two miles long. Down the middle was a small ditch. The area had apparently been made many years ago because there were trees growing along the ditch.

While we were standing there, five moose walked out, nearly causing us to pass out from excitement. We ducked down, ran back, and got our two buddies. When we returned we all climbed up on the dirt pile, slowly and quietly. There were three cows, one calf, and one huge bull. He had a heavy set of antlers. We stayed there and talked about what we should do. There was no way to get any closer, and we couldn't cross that ditch, so we decided to take the shot from the dirt pile and then figure how to cross the ditch to claim our game. We all pulled up our guns and took aim, firing fifteen rounds at the moose. Occasionally the moose would stop feeding, raise their heads and look around. They didn't mind the noise of the guns or the cursing coming from the pile. I think they had full stomachs and just walked off into the woods.

After they had left and we had finished kicking ourselves, we found a twelve-foot board, placed it across the ditch, and made our way across. We paced off the distance and those animals had been six hundred yards away! Our rifles were set for deer hunting, usually a maximum of one hundred yards, so we weren't getting close. We checked the area where they had been feeding and found no blood spots. It would have been a miracle had we hit one.

It was almost dark, so we headed back for camp. Sitting around the fire that night, we decided that we would hunt this same group of five the next morning. We would cross on the board and then spread out down the middle of the field and wait for them to come out, even if it took all day. We talked about how big the moose are, compared to the little deer we were accustomed to hunting, and how we were fooled by the distance, making them appear much closer than they actually were. Even though we knew enough to aim high, we had been badly undershooting them.

Another rookie mistake: Know the lay of the land (go to class).

The next morning came. We were up and ready to go before the farmer was out of bed. We drove the two miles to where we had seen the five moose the day before. By the time we got to the ditch, it had started to rain. Dan, Ron, and I went to put the board across the ditch and Paul went to the dirt pile to check for activity. Before we could get the board across the ditch, Paul came running back to us, whispering, "There's a moose coming across the clearing." We dropped the board and ran to the dirt pile. There in plain view was a young bull about 250 yards away, walking across the clearing. We quickly decided that we'd have to shoot from there because we couldn't get across the ditch in time. We agreed we'd each have to aim high because he was from 250 to 300 yards out. We shot eight times at him and later found that we had hit him four times.

The shot that brought him down was the one that hit him in the left knee. Moose are so heavy in the front that they cannot run with that kind of injury, where deer can sometimes run on two legs. We rushed to get the board across the ditch. Ron stayed on the dirt pile to be sure the moose didn't get away before we could carefully walk to the downed animal and finish the job. We now had the fun of field dressing a 900-pound moose. Ron went back to the car to get our backpack which contained our field-dressing gear. By now it was raining harder so we set up a plastic shelter. The DNR had issued us a moose field dressing booklet when we received our license. We needed that book and had to go through it page by page. Boy, was that book bloody by the time we were done.

While we were getting the shelter set up, a whitetail yearling came within thirty feet of us, checking out what we were doing. I walked behind the fawn as it crossed the field where I came upon the little ditch in the middle of the field. I looked across the field and there I saw a big cow moose looking back at me. The cow was a lot bigger than the bull we had gotten, and she was only fifty yards away. I yelled for the other hunters to come for a look and I was surprised that my call didn't spook the cow. When my friends reached me I raised my gun, as a joke, and asked, "Should I drop her?" even though my gun was unloaded. "Hell, no!" they said. "We've got enough work ahead of us now." The cow fed for a good half hour before it left. We started to field dress the moose around 9:00 A.M., following the little booklet page by page. You should have seen the size of that animal's heart; it was as big as a football. One had to climb inside the carcass to perform some of the steps called for in the little book. It was a big job and we worked all day getting it field dressed and quartered. Then we put each quarter in a cloth bag and used a seven-by-nine-foot tarp to carry it out. We would place a quarter on the tarp and carry it to the foot of the bridge we had made. We then made a separate trip to get the head and small rack and a final trip to bring out our gear. By the time it was all accomplished it was 4:00 P.M. and we still had three hundred yards to go to move everything to the car over a road which was one big mud hole. Darkness was only forty-five minutes away and we were all tired. We'd had only one cup of pop and no food all day long; we had-n't brought any food along because we were so close to our camp—only two miles.

We saw a Jeep sitting beside a trailer house so walked over and knocked on the door. There were two workers in the trailer and we asked if they could help us get the moose to the car. They quickly said yes because they were leaving anyway. One guy jumped into the jeep and pulled it alongside the moose. We put moose quarters in the backseat and one in the front seat, but it still took two trips to move everything to the car. Without their help it would have taken us two or three hours of very hard work to get the moose out. We agreed that each of us would pay the driver $10 for his help, but he refused the money, saying he and his partner had been watching us all day and hadn't had such a good laugh for many years. He said that if we made it to town that night and stopped at the local tavern we could buy them a cold one. He also said they appreciated us coming into their area because our bringing money into the area helped the community.

Then we found that after we had loaded the moose and gear into the car, it wouldn't move. It had sunk into the mud down to the bumpers, so we unloaded the moose and pushed on it. Then we decided to go back to the camp for help from the farmer with his four-wheel-drive pickup. He was more than willing to help, so we reloaded the moose and headed back to camp, tired, hungry, thirsty, a proud group of hunters.

We got cleaned up, put on dry clothes, and went to town to call our wives and find the guys who had helped us out and buy them a couple of cold ones. They had to tell all the customers in the place about the good time they had watching the city folks play in the rain. The next day we used the farmer's pickup to go register the moose. We went back to our camp, got the car, and drove fifty miles into Thief River Falls to rent a trailer. There were none available in the whole town for a one-way rental. We went to the local Chevy dealer to see about getting air shocks put on the car, where we were told the shocks would have to be ordered. That would take two days and would cost about $250. We decided to return to our camp to pack the car as efficiently as possible to make it home without either the air shocks or a trailer.

We packed our heavy gear as far forward as possible and put

the four moose quarters atop the car, also as far forward as we could. The bumper was still only a couple of inches off the ground.

We thanked the farmer for everything and started home. We had to slow down whenever we came to a bump or a dip in the road or the car would bottom out. We made it home and have had many good discussions about this, our first moose hunt with all the mistakes we made.

We now consider ourselves experienced moose hunters. I would give this advice to anyone thinking of applying for a moose hunting license, "Go for it! It's a once in a lifetime experience."

"But plan, plan, plan. Don't be rookies."

GARY A. JOHNSON
Columbia Heights, Minnesota

The Coolest Thing I Have Ever Seen

Over a lifetime of hunting and fishing I have retained a mental list of what I call "the coolest things I have ever seen."

Among those events are a bull elk bugeling while I sat eighteen yards away watching the show, turkeys in full strut, a muskie hitting on the figure eight, and whitetail bucks fighting.

This fall, 1995, I saw something I think will never be topped. It's such a wild story that many people will have their doubts and think I'm full of it. But I swear on a stack of Bibles that it is true.

I was on a South Dakota deer hunt over the Halloween weekend. I had been hunting for a few days and had found an area with plenty of deer signs. My stand was near a fence crossing and I had climbed into that stand for the first time, just before first light. It was an extremely beautiful morning and as daylight came I could see the fresh light snow covering the ground.

It didn't take long for the action to begin. I caught movement to my left and saw a buck coming toward me at a fast pace, I readied my bow and when the buck stopped briefly at the fence, I let my arrow go. I saw the hit was too far back and was immediately thankful for the fresh snow, thinking I might have to do some tracking. Believe me, I was pleasantly surprised when he fell in sight of me, a hundred yards away. Through my binoculars I could see he was down for good but decided to wait for thirty minutes because of the bad hit.

As it turned out, I had made the right decision because the buck got to his feet after fifteen minutes, walked parallel to my stand, and fell again after thirty yards. I decided to wait another hour.

Only a few minutes had passed when six does and a fawn came from the direction from which the buck had come, and all jumped the fence. As I watched, spellbound, they walked in single file to the downed buck. At that point the does ran in my direction; I was confused at why they had done that until I saw six small pointers, which had come from the other direction and had started chasing the does.

The does didn't show much interest in the bucks and, after a few minutes of harrassment, tired of being chased, they left the area. The two young bucks then walked over to "my" prone buck, which I wasn't sure was alive or dead. I worried that they would get my buck up and moving away, but little did I know the fun hadn't even started. The two bucks continued walking within a few feet of the older buck. I watched through my binoculars, hoping for the best. Then the first buck caught the scent of my deer. He cautiously approached the downed animal and checked him over with his nose. When my buck didn't move, I gave a sigh of relief, being assured he was dead.

When the second young buck came to investigate, the first one lowered his head and chased him off, then returned to the dead buck. He started smelling him again when, to my surprise, started fighting with the dead buck. He really started to go at it as I watched through my binoculars. He was pushing and dragging the buck in one direction, then in the other, stopping only briefly to chase away the other buck when he moved in too closely.

He fought with the dead deer for nearly ten minutes. Midway through the action the other deer started making a series of scrapes around the dead buck.

I was in a state of awe watching events unfold.

As fast as it had started, it ended. The bucks got in a single file and walked toward my stand. They passed fairly close to my stand and circled back toward my deer. As they came back to the downed deer, the same one again started fighting with my downed buck, again stopping his assault only to chase away the other young one. The two of them locked antlers near the downed one, forcing them both to their knees. Then, in an instant, the first buck took control and forced the second one to retreat.

He then returned to the dead deer and was more violent than he had been before. He reared up on his rear legs, lifting his front feet off the ground two feet or more before slamming head first into the older animal. He then picked up the dead deer, set him on his rear end and slammed him to the ground. Then he walked to the rear end of the dead one and made a scrape near the body.

After making the scrape he started toward my stand, with the other buck who had been watching from a distance following directly behind him. Again they passed close by my stand to jump the fence on the other side of the tree. Then they winded me! I have never seen deer hightail it away as fast as they did after getting my scent.

With the bucks gone I checked the time. Nearly an hour and a half had passed since I shot the buck. The two six-pointers had spent nearly an hour around the dead one.

When I think about that morning many things come to mind. I think of the beauty of the morning, of the fresh snow in the woods, the shot I made on the deer, the number of animals I saw in such a short period of time, the bucks, and how they reacted to the dead deer.

It was definitely a day to remember and certainly a hunt I will never forget.

ELLIOTT SMITH
Sibley, Iowa

Downed Deer Was Already Tagged

During the Wisconsin 1944 deer hunting season, which was a long time ago I'll admit, our group was making drives near our farm in northern Wisconsin.

One of my brothers, who was a driver, jumped two bucks, dropping one, tagging it immediately, then proceeded to search for the second, which he thought he had wounded. When he was about fifty yards away from the downed buck he had just left, he heard a commotion and, looking back, saw that the tagged buck was up and running.

We immediately rounded up the entire hunting party and proceeded to track the runaway deer. It was finally recovered and, as one of the hunters said, "There's no doubt as to whom this deer belongs to. It's already tagged."

FRAN BALSIS
Lakeville, MN

A Quadriplegic Bowhunter Finds a Way

I grew up in northwest Iowa hunting with my family and friends. I enjoyed all types of hunting but, by the time I was sixteen, bow hunting for deer became my biggest addiction.

In July 1980, when I was nineteen years old, I had a diving accident in the Apple River in Wisconsin. This injury left me a high-level quadriplegic, with no use of my arms or legs.

My paralysis did nothing to discourage my bow hunting desires. Even initially, in the hospital, I was thinking about ways that a crossbow could be adapted so that I could bow hunt again. It took four or five years of trial and error to build a crossbow that I could take into the woods. This crossbow had many bugs, and it took a few years of modifications to make it a successful bow hunting weapon. Since that time, I've taken whitetail deer, antelope, and a black bear.

As you might imagine, the outdoors are very seldom wheelchair accessible. Finding a good place to hunt is always a big challenge. Typically, I like to hunt in places where agricultural trails and game trails meet. These areas work well because I can drive my van near them and, with minimal effort, I can set up my ground blind. While I'm getting all set up in the ground blind I leave the van running because the engine noise helps cover the noise we might make as we get ready. Once we're all set, someone will drive the van away for us. Over the years I have found that the animals seem to react as if a farm vehicle came, stopped for a while, and simply drove away.

Because of my level of injury, I need to have someone nearby while I'm hunting. My wife, Heidi, also enjoys bow hunting, so quite often we will sit together in the same area. This works very well because I'm limited to a forty-five degree angle in front of me, so Heidi can cover all the areas I cannot.

We also have good friends in western Minnesota with whom we bow hunt quite often. One of our friends, Kris, is also disabled, having had arthritis most of his life. The hunting land works well for us because the terrain is very flat. The Yellow Medicine river runs through this hunting area, with ten to twenty yards of woods on each side of it. Dan, our friend who

farms the land where we hunt, has set aside into the Conservation Reserve Program (CRP) twenty yards of this farmland,
which borders the woods.

The CRP program sets aside land that the government subsi-
dizes for the environment. (Editor's note: As I understand it this
land is usually set aside for periods of ten to twenty years.) For
Dan, this keeps any chemicals from reaching the river and also
keeps his crops from competing with the trees for moisture. This
CRP strip of land creates a unique and accessible hunting opportunity for someone like me. The deer also like to use this land as
they come out of the woods and eat at the edge of the crops.
Quite often we will sit in the cornfield and face the woods, or sit
in the woods and face the cornfield. When we do see deer, they
are usually within twenty yards.

Dan, Kris, and some of the neighbors have tried to maintain a
quality deer management program. They try not to shoot any
bucks unless they feel they are in the trophy category. Several
times they have let small bucks walk right into their stand just to
get an opportunity at shooting a doe. This has increased the
number of adults they see in the area. Last year (1994) Heidi
shot her first deer, which happened to be a trophy buck. Over
the years, Dan and Kris have also shot trophies.

The bucks are always more visible and huntable as the peak of
the rut approaches. Usually, during that peak, the weather is cold
enough that my disability doesn't allow me to hunt. So in all my
years hunting from my wheelchair, I've never seen a trophy-class
buck.

One evening in mid-October 1995, Dan took some time
away from his farm work to help Heidi and me get set up in a
blind. That night, the wind was perfect for a river crossing blind
that we like to hunt. It's located not more than a couple of hundred yards from the back of his barn. It is a very difficult place to
hunt because the deer will bed down there during the day. It is
very hard to get into the woods without disturbing them, but we
decided to go there anyway.

Sure enough, as we drove into the blind, we chased away several deer that had been bedded down in the woods. We felt we
probably had greatly decreased our chances of seeing deer. We

didn't have enough time left in the day to go to another blind, so we decided to hunt there anyway. Once we were all in place, Dan drove our van away and said he would be back to pick us up at dark.

The wind was very light that night so the woods were still and quiet. Most of the leaves had already fallen off the trees so we had good vision across the river and through the woods to the fields.

As expected, hunting was slow that night; we saw birds, squirrels, and nothing else until ten minutes before dark. At that time I spotted a raccoon wandering up from the winter. It stood about thirty yards in front of me.

For several years Dan has told us about his raccoon problem and has encouraged us to help him out if we had the opportunity. Since our hunt was basically over, I decided this would be a chance to test my accuracy and give him one more fur to sell. I took aim and fired, the shot being perfect.

Heidi laid her bow down to turn and walk a couple of yards to see what I had shot. We watched the raccoon run a short distance before he fell to the ground. I whispered to Heidi, telling her the details. It was not more than a minute later she looked over her shoulder and said she saw a deer just coming into the woods about seventy-five yards away. I was slightly sick because I had taken my only shot, and reloading my bow would make too much noise and make matters worse, Heidi's bow was on the ground behind us. We figured the deer was far enough away that it would never be closer to us before dark.

"The deer is heading our way," she said, "and I think it's a buck."

Now I was feeling much less sick, because this would surely be another small buck, which we would not shoot anyway. We would get to watch this little buck as we waited to be picked up by Dan.

"I think he might be a shooter," Heidi said as she counted the points. "Seven, eight, nine. He's a ten-pointer and definitely a trophy."

"You've got to be full of it," I said, not wanting to believe her.

"No. I'm not kidding at all. Look over your left shoulder and you'll be able to see him in a second," she whispered.

She wasn't kidding or exaggerating at all. This was a very nice ten-pointer and he was walking on a trail that would eventually put him directly in front of me at 25 yards. The buck was totally unalert and would have been as easy a shot as I've ever had. Mother Nature had him full of hormones and safety was not one of his priorities.

I whispered to Heidi, "See if you can get to your bow by using me as your cover."

She managed to get to her bow, but the buck caught some slight movement which drew his attention in our direction. We froze as he gave us a staredown; slowly he started moving away from our blind. When he was facing the opposite direction, I made a grunt sound with my mouth. This turned the buck and he came closer to us. We did this several times, but we could never get him close enough for Heidi to get a shot. The original movement he had picked up kept him from coming close enough. I think that if we had had a decoy set up, this buck would have worked it over well.

A couple of minutes later Dan drove up and I was forced to tell him about the trophy raccoon that we had just gotten.

Since that night I've been the butt of many jokes, and I'm sure I'll never hear the end of it.

For my buddies and me, hunting is more than just shooting trophies. Having an opportunity at shooting a trophy deer is just a very small part of hunting; mainly it's about being with your friends, sharing stories, and unfortunately, sometimes receiving nicknames. I have a feeling I've earned a new one for myself. Perhaps several.

OWEN ORTHMAN
Roseville, Minnesota

Owen Orthmann is a C3–4 quadriplegic with no use of his arms or legs. Over his fifteen years of being disabled he has come up with a device that allows him to bowhunt from his wheel chair.

He uses a regular crossbow that has been detached from its stock so it just uses the trigger, rail, and bow. The crossbow then is mounted on a small steel box that holds an electric solenoid as well as a pressure-sensor switch. These together sit on top of a head of a video camera tripod. Everything then sits on a steel frame that attaches to his wheelchair. The solenoid is powered by batteries from his wheelchair and the pressure sensor activates the solenoid with a breath of air. To fire this crossbow, he will aim it left, right, up or down by moving the back end of the crossbow with his chin. With the crossbow aimed, he will flip an electronic safety switch with his chin, then will inhale on a tube. The breath of air causes the solenoid to push the trigger and fire the crossbow. His crossbow has been adapted to use an electronic cocking device, so target practice takes minimal effort.

Using this device Owen has been successful when hunting whitetail deer, antelope, and black bear. He would like to share any or all of these ideas with anyone who feels they might have a need for something like this. If anyone has problems finding someone to build something like this, Owen has contacts who are willing to help. For more information, Owen can be contacted at (612) 633-2031.

Editor's note: The above paragraphs have been prepared by Mr. Orthmann and released at his request.

Big Buck Dreams

As I sit motionless for what seems to be hours, the beating of my heart sounds like a hammer hitting a steel can, my arms become numb from the weight of the gun, and I must blink rapidly to keep my vision from blurring. But they keep creeping closer, inch by inch. Will they ever get sufficiently close so I can get a good look at them? They walk through the white blankets of snow, moving so lightly its a wonder they even leave tracks, as they appear and disappear from behind trees and bushes. It's as if I were watching ghosts who didn't want to know where they want to go. I can see them more clearly now, but they must be at least fifty yards away. They creep along, nibbling at the low branches of the trees, looking around as if someone called their names. They're nervous yet they continue on their way.

Although I can feel the heat of the rising sun coming from behind me, I don't feel the ten-below-zero windchill. I can hear the blood pumping through my veins, rapidly. There they are, within twenty yards, two does and a buck. Suddenly they start walking, noses in the air. I can see the moisture gleaming off their muzzles and as quick as a wink . . .

. . . not BLAM, BLAM, BLAM, but RING, RING, RING, the sound of the alarm clock awakens me. I sit up in bed with the sweat running down my face, my heart is still pounding, and the anticipation of deer hunting season, which begins tomorrow, is almost more than I can handle. The sun is coming up, the trees are swaying, and there is still so much to do before the hunt can begin.

I go to the storage room to dig for hunting clothes so I can hang them on the clothesline, but they're not to be found. I look for my gun and ammunition but they're gone too. I look for my hunting knife, right where I left it, and it's gone too. I yell to my mom that we've been robbed.

"Call the police. CALL THE POLICE."

She calmly asks what is the matter. "What are you looking for?" she asks. I tell her I was looking for my hunting gear, exactly where I left it last year, and it's all gone. She sarcastically replies that if I were looking for those things where I left them last year, I should look just inside the front door. She then continues, telling me exactly where I can find each item, and they are precisely where she said. However, there are problems. The scope on my rifle is loose; my knife has rust on it, I have no ammunition, and my hunting clothes smell of Downy Fresh, which deer will smell a mile away.

My heart is skipping beats and sweat is forming again on my head.

Then I look at the clock and it's nearly five o'clock; I haven't bought my license yet, and it's Friday. The tension is great as I load my gear, except for the Downy Fresh–smelling hunting clothes, which I let fall to the ground on my way to the car and to town. First, I have to pound on the door of the hardware store so I can get my hunting license and ammunition. Then it's out to the range to sight in my rifle. Then when I return home it's dark again, and I have to search everywhere in the yard for my hunting clothes, which the wind has distributed everywhere. All the time I'm hoping that odor has left the clothes, but if not, I have that $25 bottle of red fox scent, which will cover any odor.

Everything is now loaded and ready to go. It is ten miles to the hunting shack and I swear I see at least twenty deer along the road. I also see six deer on the trail into the hunting shack. As I drive into the yard I see the lights are on and smoke coming from the chimney. The other guys are already there, preparing for the hunt.

As I walk through the door anxious to tell them of all the deer I saw along the roads, I am interrupted by hoots and hollers by Brother J who had just won another hand at poker. As he slides the chips toward himself, Uncle G reminds Brother J that he is a guest in the shack. You see, Uncle G, my dad, and Cousin D are the owners of this land, and Brother J, little Cousin D, and I are considered guests who must show respect and admiration for being allowed to hunt on their land. It's all in fun but, believe me, we are reminded constantly. As brother J stacks his chips and takes a couple more off Uncle G's pile while that gentleman is lighting his pipe, I see Big Cousin G reading *Outdoor Life;* Dad is smirking because he is watching Brother J steal Uncle G's chips, Little Cousin D is digging for money so he can buy more chips, and Grandpa is mixing the cards for the next deal.

Grandpa is the eldest statesman at the camp. When he begins his stories of past hunts, the cards are quiet and everybody listens. The stories go on for hours and each one is as interesting as the one before it. The young hunters listen closely and remember any important information which can help them tomorrrow, as we decide what stand we want to sit in for the hunt tomorrow morning. As the debate ends and the dust settles, Dad says we better get to bed. Each of us finds our way to his bunk while dreams of tomorrow are already filling our thoughts.

It's morning now and I slowly make my way to my stand. It's totally dark as I walk down the trail seeing visions of the big buck I'll drop today. I get to my stand, crawl up the ladder, and sit down. Within minutes the cold wind is biting at my neck and my feet feel like ice cubes. I wonder how I'll ever be able to sit here until lunchtime. Then suddenly a hot flash of blood warms me instantly. I sit there in my mind seeing that ten-point buck walk ever closer to my stand, having no idea I am there as he rummages through the woods. His thoughts are on other things, like ripping that small sappling to shreds and leaving it like toothpicks. My heart is pounding so hard I swear the buck will hear it. I slowly raise my gun, anticipating the great shot I will have when the buck gets closer. The gun gets heavier and I begin to shake and I can't hold the gun steady. The gun steadies and I'm squeezing the gun to shoot, when, suddenly, he raises his head and he looks directly at me. I hear a GRUNT, SNORT, GRUNT, GRUNT . . . and awaken as Uncle G is snoring so hard that dust is falling from the ceiling. Then the alarm clock goes off and the shack is as busy as a beehive. Dad is putting wood on the fire and preparing breakfast. Big Cousin D and Uncle G are racing for the outhouse . . . what a sight. Little Cousin D is still asleep. Brother J is loading enough ammunition in his pockets and ammo belts to fight a small war—and win. I'm taking my clothes down from the nails on the walls where they spent the night drying. I eat a quick breakfast and am off to the woods.

I must walk very quietly and be aware of my surroundings. I've walked about fifteen minutes and I see some fallen trees that would make good cover. I get nestled in and begin the hunt. I sit very still while listening to every sound. The birds are chirping, and there is a small field mouse scurrying around the underbrush where I'm sitting—smack dab in the middle of his territory. However, the little mouse doesn't seem to mind. He stops, looks at me. Is he wondering why this intruder is sitting in the middle of his home, or is he just happy to have company that isn't trying to make him into lunch? Soon there are least five little mice running around the brush. They have accepted my presence and go about their daily business. As I listen to the sounds, I hear a new sound which sends a rush of blood through my body. Leaves are being rustled and it sounds like a deer walking up behind me. The leaves are crackling and then it is quiet. Has the deer seen me? Then I hear the leaves again and I am assured I haven't been detected.

As I listen to the leaves, hundreds of deer hunting stories my dad has told me go through my mind. One in particular is about the buck who stood off to one side of Dad's stand and would rustle the leaves to see if Dad would react. Dad decided the buck was unsure about Dad's presence and what he was doing. Is this what is going on now? Is there a deer right behind me, looking at me and rustling the leaves? Then the walking in the leaves becomes louder; the deer is coming up right beside me! I prepare myself, readying for the shot; in my mind I see a huge buck. I see the movement out of the corner of my eyes and raise my gun to my shoulder to spin on the seat and get ready to shoot.

I scan the area but there is nothing there. Where has that big buck gone? As I wonder if I imagined him another movement catches my eye. I lower my sight level in preparation of the buck and realize that a little squirrel has outsmarted me. He'll have a great story to tell his squirrel buddies back in the hole in the tree. I stand up and bow in defeat. The little squirrel chatters in his best victory voice and moves on.

I go back to the shack to have some lunch. Brother J and Big Cousin D are discussing the deer that Brother J shot this morning. The two were walking to their stand when a couple of deer came across the river, out of the brush about seventy yards away. Cousin D says he guided Brother J just like a teacher until the shots rang out and the deer fell to the ground. Brother J has another version of the story and I'm sure the debate about who is right will go on forever. I eat a quick lunch and decide to take a short nap.

After my nap I walk down the trail and try to decide where I am going to sit until dark. The sun is shining and it is a very warm afternoon. Today I brought with me a buck call. Expert hunters swear that they work but I'm still skeptical. At the end of the trail I walk along the river, following a beaver trail where the walking is easy. I still have no idea where I am going. Then I cut into the woods, remembering an old tree stand not too far away, which I have decided would be my destination. I reach it, crawl up, and settle in the stand. I put the buck call to my lips and sound three low grunts. Something is coming through the brush; it sounds like a pig grunting. Then I see the horns emerge from the brush, followed by the body of a big buck. I raise my gun and wonder how to shoot a deer which is running straight towards me with his head down.

I place the cross hairs of my scope on his left front shoulder and squeeze the trigger.

The shot rings out in the woods, and the deer stumbles to one side but continues to run. Is this another dream, like all those others? Will I have to go back to the shack and tell the others that I missed a fine, big buck? But I know I hit him because he stumbles from the shot. Or will this be another how-the-buck-dodged-the-bullet-and-is-still-laughing-at-me story, like that little squirrel?

I get out of the stand and look for any sign of blood. Darn it. There is no blood, so I follow the trail the way I think the animal went. There is no way that I missed, but it all seems like a bad dream again. The woods are quiet and there is no way of knowing that this isn't a dream. With my head down, looking for any sign of blood, I nearly stumble over a mound of dirt. As I raise my head, I realize it isn't a mound of dirt. It's an eight-point buck.

I had hit him. It isn't just a dream of a missed opportunity. As I stand over him, grasping his rack in my hand I realize that I have a big buck story which will last a life time.

And next year's hunt will be another opportunity for Big Buck Dreams.

GARY MINNIE
Twin Valley, Minnesota

Sportswoman Bags Trophy Buck*

She bagged her first deer on Sunday, November 6, 1994, at approximately 7:45 A.M.

The story though is just great! She had hunted deer approximately four years and was introduced to the sport by her father. It has always been a family tradition and she has always had a love for the outdoors.

The interesting thing about this lady is she has already beaten the odds from a near-fatal car accident which left her right arm and hand useless for some time. She now can use her right arm and just recently had surgery to fuse the bones in her wrist and break her thumb and put it in a cast to be able to have some use of her right hand.

She asked her uncle if she could hunt his property and of course he approved. He recommended that she put herself on a "stand," on a ridge approximately twenty yards off a railroad track along a stretch of grass along a fence line to swamp and small wood lots.

He told her that quite often hunters drive the deer out of the main woods and they go to the seclusion of the swamp or in the wood lot.

So, she got prepared to go hunting *alone!* She was up at 5:00 A.M. Saturday morning, on the stand by 6:00 and sitting on her mop pail waiting for a possible chance of a lifetime. Well, after sitting there all day Saturday, she finally saw a doe just before sundown. She got quite excited when she saw the doe, thinking that a buck might be close behind. That did not prevail this day.

Her persistence paid off on Sunday! Again up at 5:00 A.M., at stand 6:00 A.M., sitting on mop bucket smoking a cigarette, having a can of pop, she saw a deer coming down through a grassy area from the main woods to a swamp near the cornfield. She realized that this was her chance. It was a buck! She had been sitting in the stand that morning praying, saying, "Please God, let me have a chance at a nice buck," . . . it happened! Approximately forty yards away the deer trotted by her. She took her bolt action shotgun, loaded with a rifled slug, and took aim behind the shoulder, bracing the gun on her right arm (on the cast she had from the operation to fuse her wrist and thumb in place), pulled the trigger, and the buck took off running.

The buck ran down the fence line around the corner of the cornfield. She didn't wait as you normally should if you feel you made a killing shot. She wasn't sure she had hit the buck. Then she saw the buck lying down approximately forty yards away. She was just about to shoot again when the buck got up and ran into the cornfield. She ran to the other end because he appeared to be heading back to the main woods. She could see the corn separating toward her and was ready to shoot again when he suddenly stopped and laid down. She then crept into the corn, row by row, getting closer to the buck. Suddenly she could hear him breathing heavily (as she had made a perfect lung shot) and then heard his head hit the ground with a thump.

She crept up slowly until she saw the body of the deer and approached cautiously, punched the deer with the gun barrel, and it didn't move—then again, and it still didn't move. Finally, she went toward his head and pushed it with the gun barrel. The trophy buck was hers. She didn't realize how big he really was. She was ecstatic. She then proceeded to dress out the deer and mark the spot with her orange hat as to where he was lying so she could find him when she came back with some help. She called the local meat processor who helped her load it in the truck to take to the locker plant.

For the record, the deer weighed between 235 and 240 pounds field dressed. With a rack approximately twenty-four inches wide inside, side to side, and with twelve-and-a-half-inch main tines. She had to wait approximately sixty days for the rack to dry out before it could be measured for Boone & Crockett scoring.

On a light note to this story, she met with the family deer party that evening talking about her huge buck with the boys and she forgot that her husband, Mike, had supper waiting; it got burned and ruined because she was swapping stories with the boys. Her husband is quite a hunter, but does not hunt deer. I asked her if she planned on going again next year. She said, "Definitely will be on my agenda."

NAME WITHHELD
Minnesota

* Courtesy of the Farmington, Minnesota, *Independent*, by special permission of publisher Doug Heikkila.

A Daughter and a Son – Also Bow Hunters

When my daughter, Tricia, was about ten-years-old, she showed more than average interest in deer hunting, so I decided to take her along on a bowhunting outing one warm Indian summer day. It was a particularly warm day and having only one portable stand I lifted her up to sit in a crotch of a tree. At this point I should explain that she has unbelievable luck with wildlife. She will catch the biggest or sometimes the only fish of the day. Wildlife seems attracted to her.

We began seeing deer moving through the woods and out to an alfalfa field. It was the time of day we call "deer time," when you don't want to breathe much less make a sound. It was at that precise moment that Tricia fell out of the tree, ripping her pants about two feet down one leg. I could see that she wasn't hurt, but the part that stays in my memory is that she didn't spook the deer. In fact, a small 6-point buck began to come Tricia's way from the field, investigating the noise.

I thought "This could only happen with Tricia."

None of the deer spooked until I came down from my stand. To Tricia it was like everything else—no big deal.

When my son had reached twelve he began bowhunting with me. Now this was my second year and I hadn't gotten a deer yet.

We had just arrived home here in Brainerd, from Minneapolis, and it was now 5:00 P.M. My son wanted to go hunting, but I knew that by the time we were dressed it would be far too late to hunt. At 5:00 P.M. we should have been in our stand, alert and ready. He begged and pleaded, so I gave in and we went.

I put him in a new area I had scouted earlier and went to my stand. When I got up in my stand my cap fell to the ground, so I went down to get it. Then, while notching an arrow, the arrow slipped out of the arrow rest and holder and fell to the ground. I began looking around, hoping no one was watching, and started climbing back up to the stand and noticed that all the climbing up and down had loosened a couple of screw-in steps; I had to reposition them, thinking there couldn't be a deer within a mile of me now.

I finally got settled and was smirking to myself how crappy things had gone when my son came running across the bean field hollering. I thought "This is it. We're going home."

But he came up to me and said "I got one" and started running back to his stand. I said, "Are you sure you hit it? Did you hang something in the brush showing the direction he went? Is there a blood trail?"

All he could say was "I got one. I got one. I got one." . . . and continued running back to his stand.

When I got to his stand I found some facial tissue tied to the brush. I followed the blood trail for about fifty yards and there was my son kneeling by a 120-pound doe; he was smiling from ear to ear. I was speechless as, once again he said, "Dad, I said I'd got one."

The years have gone on and I could fill volumes on bowhunting blunders. They would bring tears to your eyes, but this last season, the last day was a dandy.

I moved out of Brainerd and bought a small place with thirty-four acres on which I hunt. My son hunts only on weekends because of his job. The following story was about the last day of bowhunting in 1994. I worked until midnight the night before and when I got up my son was here. I didn't expect him that day and told him only one portable stand was up. He asked where it was and I told him it was his and he said, "Good, looks like you get one of those rifle stands that have been there for a hundred years. I'm 6'5" and weigh 250 pounds. I wasn't relishing the idea; it was getting late so we took off.

I left my son at the portable and tried to pick a stand I thought was the sturdiest. I began to climb up when the third step from the bottom broke completely. I thought to myself that I would have to remember to be cautious at that spot when I climbed down.

Later, up in the tree at my stand, I realized I had to get down to go the bathroom. So, with an ample supply of TP in my pocket I started looking for a good brush pile. As I was descending the rickety steps I did remember the third one from the bottom was gone; that occurred to me just as I was on the top step and the second from the top came off. I slipped and held on for dear life, riding the remaining steps to the ground. At the bottom my body came to a sudden abrupt stop but my insides continued to travel at a high rate of speed and I realized I had soiled my clothes. At the nearby brush pile I cleaned myself up. My son wouldn't believe me, saying, "You what? At forty-five-years of age you did it in your pants." He continued well ahead of me as we returned to the house. Back there he asked when was the last time I changed the cat's litter box. I told him I had done it today, but what he smelled was me. He didn't change his clothes or anything; he just went home.

Bad news travels fast. When I got to work the next day I found that my fellow workers had cut out many Pampers coupons and put them in my locker as well as a roll of toilet paper wrapped around my computer and everyone stayed downwind of me.

The most important thing I will always remember is about the many times my son and I stepped out of the woods to a huge harvest moon and the feeling we got when we walked across the field together to the truck at the end of a day's hunt. It can't be put into words.

JIM ALBIE
Brainerd, Minnesota

It's a Family Affair

It hardly seems fair. The time I spend getting everything and everyone ready for the season—and who gets the big ones? I'm the guy who blazes walking trails through our hunting ground and plants the trails in clover. I work improving the habitat for wildlife. I groom the trails. I scout the territory the year around. I build stands for our hunters, and who gets the big ones? The girls.

My wife, Deb, is a hunter; she has harvested many whitetails over the years; she field dresses most of her own deer. (I've watched her attack enough carcasses, especially bucks, to know that I will be obedient and behave myself at all times.) Our sixteen-year-old daughter, Staci, has also developed a desire to hunt. Over the past two years they have become hunting partners. And me? I'm just the guy, like every good husband, who will do everything in his power to make their hunt a success.

For example, this year I built Deb her very own outhouse. I built it last spring while she was away with my oldest daughter at a convention in San Francisco. She returned the day before Mother's Day and I waited until Sunday morning to give it to her as a Mother's Day gift. I was going to wrap a ribbon around it and go through the ribbon-cutting ceremonies, but I was afraid she would get too emotional (if you know what I mean). I would have to say she was a bit more surprised than impressed, but my heart was in the right place.

Deer hunting has become a tradition in our family. Every year brothers, sisters, nephews, nieces, and in-laws show up at my mother's house. Mom's house makes a nice hunting base. It's a five-bedroom home nestled in oaks and pines, complete with free daycare, dining service, food, VCRs, pool table, and whatever else we need. The only thing Mom does not provide is moral support for the hunters. She is on the deer's side. For every deer we have ever brought home we get scolded, lectured, or at least a how-could-you? look. Every deer, every year, for thirty-five years! We wish she would quit giving us that look, but her chili is too good for anybody to complain too loudly. So we just sit and take it—and refill our bowls.

I had taken a nice eight-point basket buck with my bow a week before rifle season; that night was a textbook experience. Three does and a buck were filtering through the pines around my stand. Two does moved through within range of my stand, but the buck moved past me at about forty yards.

Not quite the shot I wanted. I grunted with my grunt call. The buck slammed on the brakes, whirled around, and thought, "Hey! Who's messin' with my scrape?" He was determined to find the intruder and zeroed in on his scrape eighteen yards from my stand. I waited until he got there and Whap! butterfly chops in the freezer. (Oh, yeah. I forgot to mention that I cook most of the venison in our house.)

We are not a greedy bunch in our hunting party. We strive for quality of the hunt, more than the quantity. We try to let everyone in our party fill his own tag. Since I had already taken my deer I would party hunt during rifle season but only take another deer if times got tough, or if a monster buck attacked me while I was sitting on my stand.

So, opening morning of rifle season I found myself sitting in the stand with an empty gun. I had a bow license, a management permit, a bucks-only rifle license, and I was sitting there with an empty gun looking at two does. I thought, "What in the hell's the matter with me? I've put in all this time and I'm sitting here with more hunting licenses on me than shells." Well, we'll just let the deer pass and enjoy the morning.

Saturday passed and everyone had a deer except my wife and daughter. They'd passed up several does, holding out for horns.

About 8:30 A.M. Sunday morning nature called and I strolled over to Deb's new outhouse. As I'm using the facility, I admire the craftsmanship of this fine building. I'm so proud of this gesture of love that I would have popped the buttons off my coveralls if they weren't down around my ankles.

Suddenly I heard a nearby shot. It sounded like Deb's gun. I got out of the facility as fast as I could and immediately saw my wife aiming and firing twice more. When I got to her stand she had a nice buck down at about seventy yards. The buck had walked out to an opening and straight away from her. It had been about to disappear in the pines when she took her first shot at the back of the neck. It's unusual for her to miss at that range with the open sights of her .250/3000 Savage. A couple of years ago she brought down a spike buck at seventy yards. I had looked at that spike and had commented on what a lucky shot she had made to hit it in the head. She looked at me indignantly and said, "That's the only part I ever shoot at." This year the buck was accommodating enough to let her get another shot and put it in the freezer. It was a heavy eight-point rack with a twenty-three-inch spread.

After field dressing the deer, Deb and our daughter decided to sit together in the same stand from which Deb had just shot her deer. I wandered off and started planning things that needed to get done before the next season.

When I returned to their stand two hours later, they had another dandy eight-point buck dressed out. Our daughter had brought it down with one shot from her .243 Ruger.

The hunt was complete.

It was a perfect weekend.

Of course, since the girls got the big ones, I had to put up with some ribbing from friends and family. Everyone in our party had shot his own deer. Everyone was done until next year. Everyone except me, of course. There were new trails for me to blaze and new habitats to develop.

So, back to how I started the story.

It doesn't seem fair. It just doesn't seem fair that I get to have all the fun getting ready for hunting and all they get to do is shoot the deer. As my brother, Dan, so accurately stated it, "When we look back and talk of the good ol' days, we will be talking about now."

Bob Sieling
Bertha, Minnesota

Index